wordslut

/wɝdslʌt/

wordslut

a feminist guide to taking back the english language

amanda montell

HARPER WAVE

An Imprint of HarperCollins*Publishers*

HarperCollins books may be purchased for educational, business, or sales promotional use. For information, please email the Special Markets Department at SPsales@harpercollins.com.

FIRST EDITION

Designed by Bonni Leon-Berman
Illustrations by Rose Wong

Library of Congress Cataloging-in-Publication Data has been applied for.

ISBN 978-0-06-286887-9

19 20 21 22 23 LSC 10 9 8 7 6 5 4 3 2 1

For B, C, and D
And in loving memory of E ♥

contents

meet sociolinguistics

what all the cool feminists are talking about

When I say the word *bitch*, what comes to mind? Let me guess: that girl you went to high school with—the one with the small nose who wore Britney Spears perfume and never invited you to her house parties. No?

wordslut

Then perhaps the word *bitch* conjures images of an old boss, or a roommate, or some famous she-villain like Cruella de Vil, that unholy puppy-murdering shmuck. Maybe the word *bitch* instantly catapults Kellyanne Conway's face to your mind, like a jack-in-the-box straight from hell. Or maybe, if you're a literal sort, it makes you think of a female dog. No matter your species, there are just so many ways for a gal to be a bitch.

But what if I told you that eight hundred years ago, the word *bitch* had nothing to do with women (or canines, for that matter)? What if I told you that before modern English existed, an early version of the word *bitch* was actually just another word for *genitalia*—anyone's genitalia—and that only after a long and colorful evolution did it come to describe a female beast, naturally leading to its current meaning: a bossy, evil, no-fun lady. What if I told you that this process of a totally neutral or even positive word devolving into some insult for women happens in the English language all the time? What if I told you that swimming under the surface of almost every word we say, there is a rich, glamorous, sometimes violent history infinitely more dramatic than any Disney movie or CNN debate? What if I told you that without even realizing it, language is impacting all of our lives in an astonishing, filthy, and fascinating way?

Cozy up, dear reader. Because this is a book about the psychedelic universe that exists behind the English language. Words are something so many of us take for granted, which of course makes perfect sense. We start learning language straight out of the womb (truly, at six weeks old we're already experimenting with vowel sounds), and from then on, we come to wield it so naturally that we never really consider why it works the way it does. Growing up, I had no idea that there was a whole academic field dedicated to examining every infinitesimal detail of how language operates, from what your tongue is doing when you make an *r* sound to why Americans love British accents so much.*

But every part of our speech—our words, our intonation, our sentence structures—is sending invisible signals telling other people who we are. How to treat us. In the wrong hands, speech can be used as a weapon. But in the right ones, it can change the world. That may sound melodramatic, though I promise it isn't. Take it from a language scholar at the University of California, Santa Barbara named Lal Zimman, who told me that one of our culture's biggest obstacles is the idea that language doesn't matter the way that other, more tangible forms of freedom and oppression do. It's that old mythology that sticks and stones may break your bones but words can never hurt you. "Getting people to understand that language itself is a means through which people can be harmed, elevated, or valued is really important," Zimman says.

---

* This, by the way, has to do with a fetish for the exotic, plus a set of mommy issues that colonial countries tend to have with their motherlands. Hypothetically, if Martians established colonies on Venus, you can almost guarantee the Venusians would find a Mars accent super sexy.

wordslut

Zimman, like most of the other word whizzes I talked to for this book, is a linguist, a profession that (despite common misconceptions) has nothing to do with learning to speak dozens of foreign languages or correcting people's split infinitives. Linguistics is, in fact, the scientific study of how language works in the real world. Under that umbrella falls sociolinguistics, where the studies of language and human sociology intersect. It actually wasn't that long ago (around the 1970s) when linguists first began studying how human beings use language as a social tool to do things like create solidarity, form relationships, and assert authority. Out of everything they investigated, the most eye-opening and contentious subject has undoubtedly been language and gender—that is, how people use language to express gender, how gender impacts how a person talks, and how their speech is perceived. Over the decades linguists have learned that pretty much every corner of language is touched by gender, from the most microscopic units of sound to the broadest categories of conversation. And because gender is directly linked to power in so many cultures, necessarily, so is language. It's just that most of us can't see it.

Speaking of power, you may or may not have heard of a little thing called patriarchy: a societal structure in which men are the central figures. Human societies haven't always been patriarchal—scholars believe man's rule began somewhere around 4000 BCE. (Homo sapiens have been around for two hundred thousand years in all, for context.) When people talk about "smashing the patriarchy," they're talking about challenging this oppressive system, linguistically and otherwise. Which is relevant to us because in Western culture, patriarchy has overstayed its welcome.

It's high time the subject of gender and words makes its way beyond academia and into the rest of our everyday conversations. Because twenty-first-century America finds itself in a unique and turbulent place for language. Every day, people are becoming freer than ever to express gender identities and sexualities of all stripes, and simultaneously, the language we use to describe ourselves evolves. This is interesting and important, but for some, it can be hard to keep up, which can make an otherwise well-meaning person confused and defensive.

We're also living in a time when we find respected media outlets and public figures circulating criticisms of women's voices—like that they speak with too much vocal fry, overuse the words *like* and *literally*, and apologize in excess. They brand judgments like these as pseudo-feminist advice aimed at helping women talk with "more authority" so that they can be "taken more seriously." What they don't seem to realize is that they're actually keeping women in a state of self-questioning—keeping them quiet—for no objectively logical reason other than that they don't sound like middle-aged white men.

More troubling still, there are also plenty of folks—usually ones of some social privilege—who want to stop language from evolving at all costs. These are the grumps

wordslut

you may find dismissing gender-neutral language as ungrammatical, refusing to learn the difference between sex and gender, or lamenting the inability to throw around the word *slut* willy-nilly without being called sexist, like they could in the good old days. Sensing the grounds of linguistic change quaking beneath them, these humans take phenomena like vocal fry and gender-free pronouns as a spine-chilling omen that their dominance in the world is at stake. So they dig their heels in, hoping that if they can keep English as they know it from changing—a futile effort, as any linguist will tell you—the social hierarchies that they so benefit from will remain intact.

We're living in an era when many of us often feel overwhelmed and silenced by the English language. But it doesn't have to be that way. We can take it back. And in this book, you're going to learn how.

But first: a history lesson. Because taking back the English language can't work unless we know where it came from in the first place. Can't cure a disease unless you figure out what causes it, you know? The good news is that the English language was not literally invented by a group of white dudes in robes sitting in a room deciding on the rules (though sometimes that is very much the case, like in France—more on that later). For the most part, however, that's not how language works. Instead, it develops organically.

To get us started on this linguistic journey together, allow me to present a brief time line of how the English language was born.

In the fifth century AD, a trio of Germanic tribes from Scandinavia called the Angles, the Saxons, and the Jutes show up at the British Isles unannounced. (Maybe they arrive nicely, maybe they arrive violently; historians aren't totally sure—but judging by their sharp metal accessories, I'm willing to wager a guess.) These tribes speak a language called Englisc, which kind of sounds like a troll language from *Lord of the Rings,* with lots of rolled *r*'s, dark vowels, and throaty, phlegmy consonants. This lingo, along with the north Germanic languages spoken by Vikings (who came a few centuries later), pushes Britain's Celtic languages to the outskirts of the country. The little bit of Celtic that's left behind combines with these other guys' languages to eventually become what we know as Old English (totally incomprehensible today, unless you're an Old English scholar, in which case, hello and welcome, fellow nerd).

Old English is spoken in Britain until 1066 AD, when the Duke of Normandy (aka William the Conqueror, aka a terrifying little man with a long, gray beard and a fabulous bejeweled crown) invades England, murders a bunch of people, and brings along with him an early form of French. For the few hundred years that follow, there is a sort of linguistic class divide in Britain, where the poor speak English and the rich speak French. But then the black death sweeps through and kills off about a third of the population. This makes the working class way more important to the country's economy, and by the fourteenth century, English is the

wordslut

dominant language of Britain again. But at this point, the language, heavily influenced by French, has evolved into a new form called Middle English (which you've probably seen in the swirly fonts of Chaucer's *The Canterbury Tales*).

A few hundred years go by, and then a linguistic phenomenon known as the Great Vowel Shift begins. Within less than a century, vowels get significantly shorter (in fact, they're still in a process of shortening), *es* at the ends of words become silent, and the overall sound of the English language changes dramatically. Also by the 1500s, the travel-enabled British have started mingling with loads of different people and languages around the world, and this influences English too. So does the European Renaissance, during which there is a resurgence in the desire for education, a decline of the feudal system, and the invention of new technologies—the most important being, with regard to language anyway, the printing press.

The printing press is a big deal, and thanks to this snazzy new ability to mass manufacture newspapers and books, literacy increases; that, in turn, creates a need for a new standard language to print. So spelling and grammar are streamlined, and ultimately, the dialect of London, where most of the publishing business is headquartered, becomes the standard form of English. According to that standard, the first English dictionary is published in 1604 (it contains only 2,449 words; for perspective, Webster's Third New International Unabridged Dictionary, addendum included, boasts a whopping 470,000).

It's around this time in the early 1600s when colonization of North America takes off, and America's own dialect of English, influenced by French and Spanish colonists as well as the West African slave trade, eventually follows. Then the industrial revolution and technology happen, and with the innovation of new stuff and ideas (from steam engines, dynamite, and vaccines to computers and the internet), tons of new words enter the lexicon. Within a few hundred years, modern American English is born.

You may or may not have noticed, but most of the main characters in this story are men: the army dudes, the aristocracy, the merchants and laborers, the printers, the dictionary makers, the industry and technology folks. Because we live in a society where, historically, it hasn't been as easy for women to do cool things, it's been hard for them to help define the world from a position of power (though, as it turns out, women do have an enormous impact on how language evolves from the bottom up, which is its own kind of power, and we'll learn all about that very soon).

The link between language and culture is inextricable: language has always been, and continues to be, used to reflect and reinforce power structures and social norms. Because old white dudes have ruled our culture for so long, and language is the medium through which that culture was created and communicated, the time has

wordslut

come to challenge how and why we use language the way we do, and how we think about it in the first place. That means questioning the words we speak every day, as well as the contexts in which we use them—because without realizing it, something as simple as an address term or curse word might be reinforcing a power structure that we ultimately don't agree with.

I asked Deborah Cameron, a feminist linguist at Oxford University and personal hero of mine, about how exactly the English language got so sexist—is it inherently that way? Fortunately, Cameron doesn't think gendered prejudices are fundamentally built into the language's DNA—its vowels, its consonants. Instead, it's the way English is habitually used that "expresses (and so reproduces) some culturally ingrained sexist assumptions." This means—good news—the English language is not *innately* biased against women and nonbinary genders; but the bad news is that its speakers have collectively consented to wield it in a way that reinforces existing gender biases, often in ways they're not even conscious of.

One of the sneakiest ways these biases show up is that in our language, as in our culture, maleness is seen as the default. This thinking manifests in countless contexts we'll explore later, but first we can consider the idea that, in a sense, *man* and *person* are oftentimes synonymous in English. "For example, if someone begins their story with 'I saw this person the other day . . . ,' chances are that hearers of that story will most often understand this unmarked 'person' to be a . . . middle-class white man until further specified," says Scott Kiesling, a scholar of language and masculinity at the University of Pittsburgh. "Men are still very often the invisible standard against which a group's language is compared."

Hinging on that idea is the pervasive assumption that many esteemed professions—surgeons,* scientists, lawyers, writers, actors (even nonhuman actors†)—are perceived male unless proven otherwise. These subtle preconceptions are reflected when we say things like *female* doctor or *woman* scientist, implying that such positions are inherently male, while models, nurses, and prostitutes are all default female.

Something analogous happens with the trend of inserting the word *man* before what we consider "girl" words: *manbun, manbag, guyliner.*‡ These words are catchy, but in the end they accentuate the idea that

---

* Perhaps you've heard this feminist riddle: "A young boy was rushed to the hospital from the scene of an accident, where his father was killed, and prepped for emergency surgery. The surgeon walked in, took one look, and said, 'I can't operate on him—that's my son.' *How is this possible?*" This scenario trips people up because if the boy's father is dead, how could he be operating on him? Few come to the conclusion that the surgeon was in fact his mother. The rare and exotic *lady* surgeon.

† I mention the nonhuman variety because of the default male thinking unwittingly expressed when people interact with animals. "Go to a zoo and listen to dozens of parents automatically referring to every random animal as 'he' when they talk to their children," says Cameron, who's even observed this with animals that are visibly female, like lionesses with no mane.

‡ *Guyliner, mansplain, shero, dykon, bromance,* and *fratriarchy* are just a few of the many memorable portmanteaus that exist in the vocabulary of language and gender. A *portmanteau*, by the way, is a play on words that blends sounds from multiple words to produce a fun hybrid. This is not to be confused with a *pun*, which exploits the meanings of two different words that sound the same, as in, "You can tune a guitar, but you can't tuna fish. Unless, of course, you play bass!"

wordslut

objects often thought to be frivolous, like makeup and handbags, are for women, and if men are expected to participate (without being shoved into a locker, that is), they must be rebranded in a macho way. Similarly, words like *mompreneur, SHE-EO,* and *girlboss* illuminate the notion that *entrepreneur* and *CEO* are not actually gender-neutral terms but are tacitly coded as male. They suggest that when a woman endeavors in business, we can't help but to cutesy-fy her title. *Mompreneur* may read as a sparkling emblem of girl power, and it certainly makes for a good hashtag, but in practice, terms like that don't quite work to undo implicit sexism in language—they reinforce it.

Gendered thinking is also encoded in our colossal vocabulary of sexualized terms for women (*ho, tramp, skank*; stay tuned for more in chapter 1) for which there is no male parallel. Even positive gendered language shapes how we see ourselves: just think of the exceptionally gendered compliments we receive as young children. "Praise for little boys is more likely to include words like *smart* and *clever*," Cameron says, "while for little girls it's more about *pretty, cute*." These patterns are so ingrained, I've even caught myself praising my two cats for the same silly accomplishment by saying "good boy" and "pretty girl." Such disparities could, and usually do, end up informing how kids (though probably not cats) see themselves for years to come.

Gender biases have existed in language ostensibly forever, but only now does English-speaking culture find itself in the position to make a language revolution actually happen. This is because for the first time in history we have both the concrete linguistic data *and* the emotional momentum to inspire tangible differences in how we talk about gender and how we perceive the speech of men, women, and everyone in between.

Compared to the centuries-old studies of physics or geology, the study of language and gender is brand-spanking new: before the 1970s, there was simply no canon of empirical data on the subject. The dawn of this field of study coincided with the second-wave feminist movement, when there was a larger political need to understand the hidden sexism in English. Anyone who was anyone in the field of sociolinguistics at the time wanted to talk about how people use language every day to create and reflect their gender. But these ideas hadn't been formally analyzed before, and linguists got a lot of things wrong. Scholars had a ton of learning to do. But by the late 1980s and early '90s, mainstream culture's urgency about feminism had dimmed, along with much of the research. (Although, there were luckily still many scholars of color making strides in feminist theory even though it wasn't academically in vogue anymore, like Kimberlé Crenshaw, who came up with the concept of intersectionality* in 1989.) Overall, progress was stymied.

---

* \ˌin-tər-ˌsek-shə-ˈna-lə-tē \: the complex, cumulative way in which the effects of multiple forms of discrimination (such as racism, sexism, and classism) combine, overlap, or intersect, especially in the experiences of marginalized individuals or groups (*Merriam-Webster*, accessed November 10, 2018).

wordslut

It's only since the mid-2010s, as interest in the gender spectrum and sexual equality have exploded back into our consciousness, that both everyday folks and linguists are asking these questions again. Like, is it sexual harassment for a male lawyer to call his female colleague *sweetie* in the courtroom? Is it possible to use the word *slut* without being problematic? Do women apologize more than men, and if so, is that a bad thing?

English speakers are hungrier than ever for these answers, giving linguists new opportunities to collect data and correct the mistakes that so many people still believe about how men and women use language. It's time for their research to spread beyond the confines of classrooms and scholastic journals and make its way to our boardrooms, brunch tables, and lawmakers' desks. Because these findings could be instrumental in the movement toward gender equality.

One of the most exciting concepts this new crop of research shows is that women possess a secret, badass arsenal of linguistic qualities that are profoundly misunderstood and deeply needed in the world right now. (Among these clever tendencies are the proclivities to adapt more quickly to linguistic change and to ask certain types of solidarity-forming questions.) By diving into the discoveries of contemporary feminist linguists, we can learn how the language we use every day operates on a structural and cultural level, and this will help us snatch it back from the forces keeping us from getting a word in edgewise.

That's exactly what I'm here to help us do.

I'm not going to talk about myself very much in these pages, but I want to take a moment to tell you a little bit about how I fell in love with this language and gender stuff in the first place. It started long before I knew anything about linguistics, when I was just a loquacious kid growing up in Baltimore, Maryland. I had long, disheveled hair and a thirst for conversation, and by three years old, I was already the most nauseatingly talkative person my parents—mild-mannered biologists at Johns Hopkins Medical School—had ever met. I grew up enchanted by language: how speaking in a certain dialect or foreign language could entirely change the way people see you; how there seemed to be infinite ways to combine words to paint a different picture in someone's head (the varying emotions you could incite in a listener depending on whether you used the word *recalcitrant*, with its daring surplus of syllables and dynamic pairing of hard and soft *c*'s, versus *stubborn*, which always called to mind the image of some fool stubbing a toe on his own obstinacy). My parents got me a thesaurus for my tenth birthday, and it continues to be my all-time favorite gift.

Then I got to college and signed up for Linguistics 101, and you can imagine my delight when suddenly there was a whole room of people just like me, all desperately curious to know why we talk the way we do. Out of everything I studied, I was most bewitched by a course called Sex, Gender, and Language. It had

wordslut

actually never occurred to me before spotting the class on NYU's registration system in 2011 that gender had anything to do with how we speak. Sure, when I was in preschool I was irrevocably labeled "bossy" after expressing that I should be the director of the class play instead of little Danny Altman. (I ended up winning, and the play was a smash—though it earned me the nickname "*Demand-a* Montell," which I put up with until middle school.) My speech had also been reprimanded for years by teachers and workplace supervisors, who thought I spoke too loudly and said *like* too much—not to mention their distaste for my premature fondness of four-letter words. But I figured, or at least hoped, that all of this was less because I was a girl and more because I produced an abnormally high volume of language in general. After all, I was, and continue to be, a wordy gal.

In my college sociolinguistics classes, I started learning about some of the subtle ways gender stereotypes are hiding in English . . . like how the term *penetration* implies (and reinforces) the idea that sex is from the male perspective. Like sex is defined as something a man does to a woman. The opposite might be *envelopment* or *enclosure*. Can you imagine how different life would be if that's how we referred to sex? If women were linguistically framed as the protagonists of any given sexual scenario, could that potentially mean that a woman's orgasm as opposed to a dude's would be seen as the proverbial climax—the ultimate goal? Questions like that blew my mind.

It didn't take long before I realized that linguistics students aren't the only people who should be learning about these ideas. It became clear: language is the next frontier of modern gender equality. We just have to help the world see it.

In the coming chapters, we're going to learn about things like the hidden sexism in your favorite insults and curse words, why talking with vocal fry and saying *like* are actually signs of linguistic savvy, and what the hell is going through catcallers' minds when they scream, "Hey, sexy!" at strangers in the street. We're going to talk about how speaking in a more gender-inclusive way is a very cool idea while being a grammar snob is not, and why the "gay voice" is a thing while the "lesbian voice" seemingly isn't. We'll discuss the history of the word *cunt*, what *gossip* really is, how language might sound if men were wiped from the face of the planet (not suggesting, just theorizing!), and what we can do with all of this information to effect real change.

We will also come across a few complex questions (like, is it actually possible to fully reclaim the word *slut*? And, will we ever put a permanent end to verbal street harassment?) that we can't answer with 100 percent certainty. At least not yet. But by the end of this book, you will have all the nerdy know-how you need to sound like the sharpest word ninja in the room. Which, I can tell you from experience, feels pretty damn good.

Here is a story of one of those experiences—a time

when just a little dash of linguistics expertise helped me convince someone from a very different background from mine, someone with their own steadfast beliefs about how women should talk, to consider a new idea. I was nineteen, working between classes at NYU as a babysitter for a professor's daughter, who attended a prep school on the Upper East Side of Manhattan. The kid was in the same grade as another girl with a mother who wore tweed skirt suits, had hair the color of a daffodil, and grew up in a family that valued proper elocution and manners above all else—principles she was intent on passing down to her own daughter.

I met this mother on the 6 train, headed downtown to Bleecker Street, where we were shepherding our respective fifth graders. After taking our seats and exchanging a few pleasantries, I scooted over to chat with the two girls, and at a point, I used the contraction *y'all* to address them: "So how did y'all's French test go?" I asked.

The tweed-clad mother did not approve. "*Y'all?*" she gasped, taking a palm to her sternum. "You *can't* go around saying the word *y'all*, Amanda. It's terrible English! People will think you're stupid . . . or worse, Southern!"* She made eye contact with her daughter and shook her head.

I live for moments like this.

---

* Fun fact about *y'all* usage: I grew up in Baltimore, Maryland, where there's a tiny bit of *y'all* happening—more so than in any state north of the Mason-Dixon line—but you don't hear it nearly as often as you would in the proper South. The state that uses it the most, according to dialect maps? Mississippi, y'all.

"Actually," I offered, sliding back across the seat, "I like to see *y'all* as an efficient and socially conscious way to handle the English language's lack of a second-person plural pronoun." The mother raised an eyebrow. I continued, "I could have used the word *you* to address the two girls, but I wanted to make sure your daughter knew I was including her in the conversation. I could also have said *you guys*, which has become surprisingly customary in casual conversation, but to my knowledge, neither of these children identifies as male, and I try to avoid using masculine terms to address people who aren't men, as it ultimately works to promote the sort of linguistic sexism many have been fighting for years. I mean, if neither of these girls is a guy, then surely together they aren't *guys*, you know?"

The mother gave me a skeptical smile. "I suppose," she said.

"Exactly!" I carried on, delighted to have been given an inch. "There are other interesting alternatives: I could have said *yinz*, which is standard in Western Pennsylvania and parts of Appalachia, but I personally don't think it rolls off the tongue quite as nicely. All things considered, I simply find *y'all* to be the most fluent solution to a tricky lexical gap. I also know that the word is highly stigmatized, as it's associated with a certain geographical region and socioeconomic background, much like the word *ain't*, which, by the way, was actually used abundantly among the English upper crust in the nineteenth century."

wordslut

"Is that true?" the mother perked up.

"It is," I confirmed. "Anyway, I'd love to learn more about your opposition to the word *y'all*. Tell me about your upbringing."

For the next ten stops, the mother proceeded to unload her whole story—her immigrant parents, the impossible elocutionary standards set for her as a child—and by the time we all stepped off the train at Bleecker Street, I was certain she'd think twice the next time she desired to chastise someone for using the word *y'all*. Part of me was confident she'd never do it ever again.

I wrote this book to help women (and other marginalized genders) feel as empowered by words as I did on the 6 train that day. To arm us all with the knowledge we need to reclaim a language that for so long has been used against us. Sick of being told how you should and shouldn't use your voice? Good news: linguists are sick of it too. This is our chance to change it.

slutty skank hoes and nasty dykes

a comprehensive list of gendered insults i hate (but also kind of love?)

If you want to insult a woman, call her a prostitute. If you want to insult a man, call him a woman.

No one is more familiar with this formula than Laurel A. Sutton, a language analyst and copywriter who has built her career on the delicate art of name-calling. In 1998 Sutton founded a "naming firm" called Catchword, a business dedicated to dreaming up zingy brand names for business owners who don't have an ear for that sort of thing. (Catchword's client list includes everyone from Allstate to McDonald's. You know the fast-food empire's famous McCafé Frappé Mocha? Catchword named that. And come up with a more appropriate name for a two-dollar, 420-calorie coffee milk shake—I dare you.)

wordslut

Five years before Sutton figured out how to monetize her flair for phonologically pleasing menu items, she was hooked on a different sort of name calling: gendered insults. In the early 1990s, Sutton was a graduate student in the linguistics department at UC Berkeley when she was struck with an unquenchable thirst for unearthing the social subtext behind America's favorite epithets. So over the course of two semesters, she conducted an experiment: Sutton had each of her 365 undergraduate students compile a list of ten slang words they and their friends used most frequently, plus their definitions. She then entered these into a giant database, like a pre-internet Urban Dictionary. Sutton's plan was to analyze the terms on the basis of gender—to find out what they said about women's and men's places in the greater cultural dialogue.

The students reported back with a veritable pupu platter of colorful words and expressions—3,788 of them, in total—on all different topics. (Remember when people used to say "booyah?" Ah, the nineties.) In total, 166 of the collected terms were either for or about women specifically. Sutton isolated these terms, looked for patterns, and was able to divide them into four semantic categories based on the following themes: sexual promiscuity, fatness, evilness, and level of hotness. Highlights from the database included words such as *slut*, *whore*, and *skankly hobag* (used to describe sexually loose women); *bitch* and *biscuit* (for women with an attitude); *hootchie* and *pink taco* (to represent a woman by describing just her genitals); and *heifer* and *hellpig* (to describe a woman based on her ugliness or unfuckability).

A similar survey of gendered insults conducted at UCLA the year before found that approximately 90 percent of all recorded slang words for women were negative, compared to only 46 percent of recorded words for men. That means there were simply more insults for females in people's everyday lexicon than there were for males. The survey also found a range of "positive" terms for women, but most of them were still sex-themed, like the insults, often comparing women to food: *peach, treat, filet.*

Before unpacking all this data, I would like to take a millisecond to appreciate the creativity of some of the terms Sutton collected (*Skankly hobag*? *Hellpig*? Such imagination). But there exists a larger issue: Why, exactly, are there so many outrageous insults for women in the English language? Also, why are some of them secretly so much fun to say? Is there a way to negotiate human beings' love for name-calling without being flat-out sexist?

Sutton is not the first linguist to take an empirical look at our language's robust canon of sexist slang. "A great deal of work has been done on the 'ugly names' for women," she acknowledges in her paper, pointing out that research consistently shows a much fuller wealth of sex- and gender-based insults for women in English than it does for men. (Linguists postulate this would also be

slutty skank hoes and nasty dykes

the case in any language spoken under a patriarchal system, since language ultimately reflects the beliefs and power structures of its culture.) In English, our negative terms for women, which usually carry sexual connotations, necessarily mirror the status of women in Western society at large—that being the status of *treats* and *filets*, at best, and *hobags* and *hellpigs*, at worst. It's a classic case of the virgin/whore dichotomy—according to our inventory of English slang, women are always either one of two types of sexual objects: an innocent hard-to-get peach or a grotesque, too-easy skank.

In the 1970s linguist Muriel Schulz was one of the first researchers to take a deep dive into these unfriendly waters. Schulz is now retired, but as a linguistics professor at Cal State Fullerton, she published an iconic paper in 1975 called "The Semantic Derogation of Woman." In it, Schulz describes *semantic change*, the process of how word meanings evolve over time, illuminating how gendered nicknames—from *cupcake* to *cunt*—came to be. There are two types of semantic change: *pejoration* is where a word starts out with a neutral or positive meaning and eventually devolves to mean something negative. The opposite is called *amelioration*.

Nearly every word the English language offers to describe a woman has, at a point during its life span, been colored some shade of obscene. As Schulz writes, "Again and again in the history of the language, one finds that a perfectly innocent term designating a girl or a woman may begin with totally neutral or even positive connotations, but that gradually it acquires negative implications, at first perhaps only slightly disparaging, but after a period of time becoming abusive and ending as a sexual slur."

The main piece of evidence for this tendency toward women's linguistic disparagement appears when you examine certain matched pairs of gendered words. Compare, for example, *sir* and *madam*: Three hundred years ago, both were used as formal terms of address. But with time, *madam* evolved to mean a conceited or precocious girl, then a kept mistress or prostitute, and, finally, a woman who manages a brothel. All of that excitement while the meaning of *sir* just stuck where it was.

A similar thing happened with *master* and *mistress*: These terms came to English by way of Old French, and initially both of them indicated a person in a position of authority. Only the feminine term contaminated over the decades to mean a sexually promiscuous woman with whom a married man, as Schulz puts it, "habitually fornicates." Meanwhile, *master* continues to describe a dude in charge of something, like a household or an animal (or a sexual submissive, if we're talking BDSM). *Master* can also indicate a person who has conquered a difficult skill, like karate or cooking. Tell me, is there a wildly entertaining television competition show called *MistressChef*? No, there is not. (I would definitely watch that, though.)

In some instances, the process of pejoration rebrands a feminine word as an insult not for women but for

wordslut

men. Take the words *buddy* and *sissy*: Today, we might use *sissy* to describe a weak or overly effeminate man, while *buddy* is a synonym for a close pal. We don't think of these words as being related, but in the beginning, *buddy* and *sissy* were abbreviations of the words *brother* and *sister*. Over the years, the masculine term ameliorated as the feminine term went the other way, flushing down the semantic toilet until it plunked onto its current meaning: a man who is weak and pathetic, just like a woman. Linguists have actually determined that the majority of insults for men sprout from references to femininity, either from allusions to women themselves or to stereotypically feminine men: *wimp*, *candy-ass*, *motherfucker*. (Even the word *woman* itself is often used as a term of ridicule. I can hear it now: "Dude, don't be such a woman.")

The word *pussy* is analogous to *sissy*, in that it's a feminine word that was gradually reduced to an insult not for women but for men. Scholars aren't 100 percent sure of *pussy*'s beginnings, but one theory is that it comes from an Old Norse word meaning "pouch" or "pocket."* There's also an *Oxford English Dictionary* entry from the sixteenth century that defines the term as a girl or woman who bears similar qualities to a cat,

---

* In season 1 of the comedy series *Broad City*, Ilana Glazer's character proudly calls her vagina "nature's pocket" after divulging her habit of discreetly transporting marijuana inside of it. And if that's not proof of the Old Norse theory, then I don't know what is.

like affability and coyness. By the 1600s, the word had surfaced as a metaphor for both a cat and a vagina. It wasn't used to describe men until the early twentieth century, when writers began associating it with tame, unaggressive males.

Few traditionally masculine terms have undergone pejoration like *sissy, pussy, madam, or mistress. Dick* is really the only prominent example—this word started as an innocent nickname for men named Richard; by Shakespeare's time it was extended to mean a generalized everyman (like a "Joe Shmoe"); in the late nineteenth century it evolved to describe a penis (which we can likely attribute to British military slang—those dirty boys); and in the 1960s it grew to refer to a thoughtless or contemptible person. *Dick*, however, is an outlier. *Lad, fellow, prince, squire,* and *butler* are just a handful of other pejoration-worthy masculine words that have been spared.

Do feminine terms ever ameliorate? They do, but it's often because women actively reclaim them (and we'll talk more about how that happens toward the end of this chapter). But finding more instances like *buddy*, wherein a masculine term gains a more positive status over time, is an easier task. An Old English version of the word *knight*, for example, simply meant young boy or servant, before ameliorating to describe a gallant nobleman. The word *stud* graduated from a term for a male breeding animal to a slang phrase for a hot, manly dude. Even the word *dude* itself has elevated in status since the late nineteenth century, when it was used as an insult to describe an affected, foppish man. Today, *dude* is one of the most beloved words in the English language.

But back to all those wacky insults for women. Because it's so fun to talk about, and such charming fodder for cocktail party conversation, I want to talk about the history of a few more of the many insults for or about women that used to mean something neutral or positive— a term of endearment, even—but at some point transitioned to mean something unflattering (and usually sexual).

Let's start with the word *hussy*. Originally this term was nothing but a shorter, sweeter version of the Old English *husewif*, which meant female head of household and is an early cognate of the modern word *housewife*. Around the seventeenth century, the word came to describe a rude "rustic" woman; then, it became a general insult for women of any kind, and eventually it narrowed to mean a lewd, brazen woman or prostitute. The word *tart* went down a similar road. Once used to describe a small pie or pastry, the term soon became an innocent term of endearment for women, then specified to mean a sexually desirable woman, and by the late nineteenth century had descended to a female of immoral character or prostitute (which, of course, despite common rationale, are not the same thing).

Even the word *slut* used to mean something relatively innocent. The word is so contentious now you'd never guess it came from the comparatively wholesome Middle English term *slutte*, which merely meant an "untidy" woman. The word was even used for men sometimes (in 1386, Chaucer labeled one slovenly male character as "sluttish"). Soon enough, though, the word extended to mean an immoral, sexually loose woman or prostitute, and as of the late 1990s, this definition has been fortified by its heavy usage in pornography. There is a male equivalent of *slut*: *manslut*. However, I think we can all agree that this word is much sillier in connotation; plus, if *slut* with no modifier is a default female term, then *manslut* surely stands to imply that promiscuity is only contemptible when women do it.

SLUTS THROUGH THE YEARS

1300s 1800s

2000s THE FUTURE?

wordslut

Cruder still, we have *bitch*, which we already discussed a bit, but just to paint the full picture: linguists postulate that this word derived from the ancient Sanskrit word *bhagas*, meaning "genitals," then later found its way (in various forms) into Latin, French, and Old English, eventually coming to refer to a creature with exposed genitals, aka an animal. After that, the word narrowed to female animal, and within a few centuries, we landed on female dog. The first shift in meaning from beast to human wasn't recorded until around 1400 AD, when *bitch* surfaced in writing to describe a promiscuous woman or prostitute (which is still one of its primary meanings in British English). From there, the word evolved to describe a sort of weakling or servant ("Go fetch me my tea, bitch"); a stuck-up, mean, unpleasant woman; and finally a verb meaning "to complain." ("There are so many English words to bitch about, aren't there?")

And yet, out of all these etymological allegories, my favorite has to be the story of *cunt*. What is largely considered the English language's most offensive term for women didn't actually start as an insult at all. *Cunt*'s roots are also up for debate, but most sources agree they can be traced back to the Proto-Indo-European word sound "cu," which indicated femininity (this same "cu" is also related to the modern words *cow* and *queen*). The Latin term *cuneus*, meaning "wedge," is also connected to *cunt*, as is the Old Dutch word *kunte*, which gives the word its dramatic final *t*. For centuries, *cunt* was used to refer to women's external genitalia without any negative nuances whatsoever; but, like so many other terms referencing femaleness, it didn't stay that way. What's particularly interesting about *cunt*'s pejoration is that it is directly linked to human history itself. Ten thousand years ago, when Homo sapiens lived nomadic lifestyles, wandering from place to place, men and women all had multiple sexual partners and female sexuality was considered totally normal and great. It wasn't until human beings stopped moving that women with sexual independence started gaining a bad rap, because once owning land became desirable, people wanted to be able to pass it down to their children, and in order for men to know who their children were, female monogamy became a must. To create a system of inheritance, societies became patriarchal, and any remaining notions of goddess-like sexual liberation went kaput. With the end of women's sexual liberation came a general disgust for female sexuality, dooming words like *cunt* forever. (Or until the end of patriarchy, at least.)

Spiritually, reading all about these words' pejoration is a bit of a bummer, but empirically, the patterns say something important about our culture's gender standards at large: when English speakers want to insult a woman, they compare her to one of a few things: a food (*tart*), an animal (*bitch*), or a sex worker (*slut*). These are the very same themes Laurel A. Sutton noticed in her study at UC Berkeley in the '90s. That we have used language to systematically reduce women to edible, nonhuman, and sexual entities for so many years is no coincidence.

wordslut

Instead, it makes a clear statement about the expectations, hopes, and fears of our society as a whole.

Since the very beginning of language, the names we use to refer to people have symbolized the history, status, and very worth of their referents. I'm not just talking about insults; this can also be applied to one's legal name (which 70 percent of American women still believe they should change with marriage, either unaware or in denial of the fact that this signifies a transfer of ownership from their dads to their husbands). When we compare a woman to a farm animal or a fruity pastry, it isn't random; it reflects what our language's speakers believe (or want to believe) to be true.

Look at our culture and our repertoire of insults for women side by side, and it's no wonder that so many of them have sexual undertones. "Woman as sex object" is one of patriarchy's oldest tropes, mostly due to that thousands-of-years-old attitude that a woman's personal desire and sexual free will are inherently bad. Even a brief scan of our language's slang for women will reveal that female desire is worthy of shame no matter what a woman chooses to do with it, which can only be one of two things per our culture's rules: having a lot of sex, which earns her the reputation of a whore, or opting to withhold it, which gets her labeled a prude. In the late 1970s, a University of Nebraska scholar named Julia P. Stanley found linguistic proof of this pervasive whore-Madonna polarity after collecting and analyzing a catalog of popular sexual slang terms for women. She recorded 220 in total, and the metaphors underlying them were both entirely negative and also fell on either side of this ideological coin: the women who "put out" were categorized as sluts, and those who didn't were damned as ice princesses. Meanwhile, most of the sexual metaphors Stanley collected for men (twenty-two in all, precisely one tenth of the set for women) had actively positive connotations. These terms, which included *ass man*, *stud*, and *Don Juan*, suggested an all-out approval of male promiscuity.

The animal and dessert metaphors often used to describe women ultimately work to reduce them to this same status of sexually reprehensible things. Likening people to animals certainly isn't anything new or exclusive to women: for centuries, people of all genders have evoked beasts both wild and domestic to describe people's habits and appearance. Women certainly compare people to animals, including other women. They have no problem calling each other *bitches* and *cows*.* They use animal metaphors for men too—they call them

---

* Although, sometimes there are big semantic differences between how women and men use the same animal metaphors. A 2013 study from the University of Belgrade in Serbia looked at each gender's usage of identical animal words to describe women, and the results were intriguing: While men used the Serbian word for *bitch* to describe "a playful woman who enjoys and readily engages in promiscuous sex," women used it to refer to "a shallow, conceited, or frivolous woman." While the word for *pig* was used by men to describe sloppy, untidy women, women used it to call other women fat. (These are just a few examples.)

pigs when they're being messy, for example, or sexually predatorial. But these are references to a person's behavior, not judgments about how willing they are to "give it up" for someone else's pleasure. By contrast, when dudes use animal metaphors for women, the symbolism often says one of a few things: that women are meant to be hunted (like a bird), subordinated and domesticated (like a kitten or a cow), or feared (like a cougar*).

But comparing women to dessert is my personal favorite pattern to analyze. Caitlin Hines, a San Francisco State University linguist, has devoted much of her research to determining the unwritten rules of how English speakers characterize other people as food. In 1999, Hines conducted an analysis revealing that women are systematically likened to sugary, fruity items like tarts and cupcakes, as opposed to more substantial "masculine" parts of the meal, like beefcakes. More pointedly, the desserts women are associated with are always, as Hines describes, "firm on the outside, soft or juicy in the middle, and either able to be cut into more than one piece (cherry pie, pound cake) or conceptualized as one (snatched) serving of an implied batch (crumpet, cupcake, tart)." You never see women compared to ice-cream cones or chocolate mousse because speakers,

---

* I love cats but I don't love how people describe women as "catty," often labeling physical and even verbal altercations between women as "cat fights" (a phrase invigorated by television shows like *The Bachelor* and *The Real Housewives*). Meanwhile, when we compare dudes to felines, they get to be "cool cats."

whether they realize it or not, recognize the rules of the "piece of ass" metaphor and adhere to them. They understand and comply: women, like tarts, are sweet, single-serving items meant to be easily snapped up.*

Here's the wrench in this whole analysis, though: men aren't the only speakers who get these rules and stick to them—women do it too. Women label each other things like *honey* and *cupcake*† all the time. They call one another *sluts*, *hos*, and *cunts* too. But why? As Schulz says, "It is clearly not the women themselves who have coined . . . these epithets for each other." (Women weren't the first to describe men as *pussies* and *sissies*, either.) So why do we go along with it? Why do so many women unquestioningly agree to use these unpleasant, dude-invented metaphors to verbally dress each other down?

I'll offer the simple answer first. In our culture, men run the show, women are taught to follow their leads, to please them, and thus we go out of our way to fit into the semantic categories set up for us: prude or whore, bitch or sweetheart, princess or dyke. But there's a slightly

---

* According to lexicographer Eric Partridge, there was a Canadian expression in the 1880s that went, "Next time you make a pie, will you give me a piece?" This, I regret to report, was something a man might say to a woman to hint that she should "sexually cooperate with him."

† They do it *slightly* differently, though: there are a few dessert-y words that can be used as gender-neutral terms of endearment or, if you're in the American South, terms of politeness (I can hear my Louisianian aunts now: "Do you need anything else, *sugar*?"). This is obviously different than if, say, a judge in a courtroom were to call a woman attorney *sugar* or *sweetie*. Context will typically reveal if a term is being used in an objectifying way or a courteous one.

more complex answer too, which says what's really going on is that women happen to be better at a thing called *listening*. Cornell linguist Sally McConnell-Ginet once argued that women, on the whole, have become better at picking up on the thoughts, feelings, and perspectives of the people they're talking to. Theoretically, that should be a good thing. But where it gets tricky is that this generally ends up giving men more space to project the particular metaphors that make sense to them all over our culture's collective vocabulary, as if their perspectives are the only ones that count.

McConnell-Ginet explains it like this: "The more one talks and the less one listens, the more likely it is that one's viewpoint will function as if it were community consensus even if it is not." The idea here is that on some level, women are aware that dudes have come to understand their viewpoint as the only one that exists and wouldn't pick up on the metaphors that represent women's positions even if they tried. If they did, *sissy* might be the word we use for a good friend instead of *buddy*, and *pussy* might be what we call, I don't know, a badass warrior queen.* But, as McConnell-Ginet says, "The more attention one pays to perspectives different from one's own, the more likely one is to give tacit— indeed sometimes unwitting—support to these other views simply by being able to understand them." Thus,

---

* As the legendary Betty White once said, "Why do people say 'grow some balls?' Balls are weak and sensitive. If you wanna be tough, grow a vagina. Those things can take a pounding."

women's experiences wind up getting squashed under their own generosity as listeners.

These dude-invented perspectives about men and women slip into the subtext beneath so many insults, even ones that aren't explicitly gendered. Think of terms like *nasty*, *bossy*, and *nag*: though there are no overt references to femaleness in these words, they have fallen into a class of insults reserved for women alone. In 2017 sociolinguist Eliza Scruton conducted a study in which she examined a corpus (that's a large collection of language samples) containing more than fifty million words from the internet to determine exactly how gender-specific words like *nasty*, *bossy*, and *nag* really are. In short? Very. Her data revealed that these terms skew strongly female in usage, often appearing before the words *wife* and *mother*.

Chi Luu, a computational linguist and language columnist at JSTOR Daily, once made the point that the purpose of name-calling is to accuse a person of not behaving as they should in the eyes of the speaker. The end goal of the insult is to shape the recipient's actions to fit the speaker's desired image of a particular group. *Nasty* and *bossy* criticize women for not behaving as sweet and docile as they ought to—for wanting too much power. Equally, words like *wimp* and *pansy* point out a man's failure to live up to the macho standard of what men are supposed to be. In a culture that places such importance on men being tough and aggressive, and women being dainty and deferential, having someone accuse you of doing your gender badly often feels like the worst insult of all, because it tells you that you've failed at a fundamental part of who you are.

Gendered insults are damaging because they work to propagate harmful myths about men and women, which is not great for equality. So we should just give them up altogether, right? As it turns out, not exactly. As much as I hate being called a *bitch* in the middle of a fight, that doesn't explain why I, and many other women, actively delight in so many of the gendered terms I've listed in this chapter. Personally, I proudly identify as *nasty*, a *bitch*, and a *slut*, which are also names that my friends and I would happily call each other with affection. And I'm only partially ashamed to admit that I also find words like *tart* and *hussy* just plain fun to say.

On the surface, these predilections might seem like treachery to feminism, but I think most linguists would pardon me. That's because many of these slurs for women are lovable by design, simply because of how they sound. Phonetically, *slut*, *bitch*, *cunt*, and *dyke* happen to possess the essential aural recipe shared universally by English speakers' favorite, most used, and sometimes very first words. Like *mama*, *dada*, and their derivatives, our most prevailing English slang, including the terms *boob*, *tit*, *dude*, and *fuck*, tend to be short and plosive. Stop consonants like *b*, *p*, *d*, and *t* are humans' favorites from birth (if you've ever been around a babbling baby, you know this), and we continue to love them over the course of our lives. The more fun a word is to say, the likelier it is to persist; and, since terms like *slut* and *bitch* have all the acoustic trappings of a fun word, it makes sense that they'd have such staying power. It's not as if women are just brainwashed by men to want to call each other these names—their phonetic delight is empirically proven.

But even more important than how they sound, what also makes our female-directed insults so irresistible is that many of them aren't seen as completely negative anymore. This has everything to do with reclamation— with people actively redefining what these words mean from the ground up. Some of the most triumphant instances of reappropriated slurs come from our culture's most oppressed communities. Take the word *queer*, for instance. Probably the most successful example in recent history, *queer* used to be exclusively a homophobic insult but has undergone a pretty impressive reappropriation by academics and the LGBTQ+ community. *Queer* is still considered problematic by some, but in the grand scheme of things, the word has evolved into a sort of self-affirming umbrella term for nonnormative gender and sexual identities. Today it can be found in contexts as lighthearted as the title of the TV series *Queer Eye for the Straight Guy* and as formal as one of the gender options listed on a job application, next to *male* and *female*.

There are also words like *bitch*, *ho*, *dyke*, and *cunt*, which are definitely still used abusively, but have also evolved as terms of endearment among women who use them inside their own groups (which is usually how a

wordslut

word's reclamation begins—it's when the rule of "I can call myself this word, but you can't" becomes more relaxed over time). Remember Laurel A. Sutton's 1992 slang study? Sutton also found that many of her young female participants called their friends *bitch* and *ho*, not as insults, but as humorous terms of affection. My experience is the same: I know I personally say things like "hey hos" and "love you, bitch" all the time.

How did this reclamation happen? In large part, we have circles of African-American women to thank for transforming *bitch* and *ho*. African-American Vernacular English (AAVE) is a rich source of slang for America's youth in general—AAVE is responsible for treasured slang terms as new as *squad*, *fleek*, and *woke*, and as old as *bling-bling*, the use of *bad* to mean good, and the phrase *24-7*. (Sonja Lanehart, a University of Texas linguist, once told me that the first time she heard a white news anchor use the phrase *24-7* on TV, she nearly spat out her drink.) The particular way some women use AAVE has been paramount in the reappropriation of gendered insults. Many speakers of AAVE are virtuosos of a form of wordplay called *signifyin'*, the verbal art of insult in which a speaker humorously puts down the listener. Over the years, this ingenious technique has caught on beyond Black communities.

There's also a specific connection between the positive redefinition of *bitch* and women in hip-hop. Since the late 1990s, Black female recording artists have used the phrase *bad bitch* to refer to a confident, desirable woman, as opposed to a mean or hostile one.* (Kudos to Trina's 1999 song "Da Baddest Bitch" and Rihanna's "Bad Bitch.") Hip-hop is also responsible for the word *heaux*, a Frencher-looking and thus chicer and more pleasant alternative spelling of *hos* that my female friends and I began using in 2017. The first place I saw *heaux* was in the title of a song that came out that year, "These Heaux," by teen rapper Danielle Bregoli (who is white, incidentally, though the idea of cleverly respelling words is another thing we can attribute to AAVE, which is no doubt where Bregoli learned to do this). *Heaux* may be nothing but a cheeky orthographic play, but it gives the word enough of a female-driven makeover that it makes it feel ever so subtly more empowering and reclaimed.

Ho and *bitch* in these contexts are used not as slurs but as signals of solidarity and liberation. Certainly there are women who aren't comfortable with these words no matter what, but for the women who are, describing themselves as bitches and hos can be a way to reject old standards of femininity. Sutton analyzes it like this: "Perhaps when we call each other 'ho,' we acknowledge that we are women who have sex and earn our own money

---

* The same cannot always be said for how men in hip-hop use *bitch*. In 2011 a pair of scholars named Terri Adams and Douglas Fuller wrote that misogynistic rap often depicts bitches as women who are "money-hungry, scandalous, manipulating, and demanding" (Snoop Dogg: "Bitches ain't shit but hoes and tricks/Lick on these nuts and suck the dick") or subordinated men (Dr. Dre: "I used to know a bitch named Eric Wright"). Men's use of the word *bitch* in hip-hop isn't *all* bad, though: for one, we have 1980s rapper Too $hort to thank for coining the term *beeyatch*, which I'm personally grateful for.

wordslut

too; and when we call each other 'bitch,' we acknowledge the realities of this man-made world and affirm our ability to survive in it. Through resistance comes redefinition."

A word doesn't have to lose its negative meanings completely to be considered reclaimed. The path to reclamation is almost never that smooth. That *queer* and *dyke* can still be used as gay slurs is not necessarily a sign that their reclamation has failed. Semantic change does not happen overnight; instead, it's a more gradual process wherein one meaning slowly overlaps another, then eclipses it. As long as the positive varieties of a word steadily become more common, more mainstream, by the time the next generation starts learning the language, they will pick up those meanings first.

Of course, while reclamation is slow-moving and mostly occurs through the daily grind of using old words in new contexts, there are a few organized efforts that can help speed things up. Activism is one of them. Look at what happened with the word *suffragette*: We no longer think of this term as an insult, but originally, it was invented as a demeaning version of the word *suffragist* (a Latin-derived term meaning a person of any gender who aims to extend voting rights). When *suffragette* was first coined, it was intended as a diminutive smear for women's liberation activists in the early twentieth century: *suffragettes* were husbandless hags who dared to want the vote. The women's lib movement was obviously far from perfect (it pretty much only benefited rich white ladies), but what was cool linguistically was that those women immediately stole the word *suffragette*, put it up on posters, shouted it through the streets, named their political magazine after it, and now most English speakers have entirely forgotten that it was ever meant as a slur.

In more recent years, we've seen activists try to replicate this sort of success: consider Amber Rose's Slut Walk, a yearly march against rape culture, or the annual Dyke March, a lesbian pride event. Certainly, lesbians have been using *dyke* to describe themselves since long before the first march was organized in the 1980s, but the image of fifteen thousand women marching through the streets with the letters *D-Y-K-E* proudly scrawled across their signs, sweatshirts, and bare breasts certainly helps the word along its way.

In the age of the internet, memes—that is, viral web symbols—have also helped transfer the ownership of a word from the abusers to the oppressed. One of the most famous examples of reclamation-by-meme has to be *nasty woman*. Less than twenty-four hours after Donald Trump uttered the *nasty woman* heard around the world during a 2016 presidential debate with Hillary Clinton, it was made into a gif, a line of mugs (I own one), and a digital fund-raising campaign for Planned Parenthood. It only took about a day for the online mob to successfully snatch the phrase from the man who first said it. The internet can sometimes be cool that way.

Now comes the fun part: knowing what we now know about how gendered insults evolved and what they accomplish, we have to figure out what to do next. How can we all proceed to make sure words like *bitch*, *slut*, and *pussy* don't continue to work for evil instead of good? How can we approach our language usage in a way that's fun and playful but also not perpetuating toxic gender stereotypes?

Feminist media mogul Andi Zeisler, who cofounded and runs Bitch Media (a nonprofit organization that has a reclaimed slur in its very title), told me that the first step we can take to reduce the harm caused by gendered insults is simply to avoid using them abusively. That is, to use them only in positive contexts ("Wow, impressive, she's a bad bitch!" as opposed to "Fuck her, that evil bitch").

Alternatively, we can give them up altogether—after all, not every insult is meant to be reclaimed.* *Slut* is one word that some feminists believe deserves to be terminated rather than taken back, simply because having a "special" word for female promiscuity is shady to begin with. Even Amber Rose, founder of the Slut Walk

---

* And not every insult that an in-group reclaims is meant for everyone's use. Take the *n*-word: from the early nineteenth century until roughly the 1980s, this word was only ever used as one of abuse, but, with the help of hip-hop artists like Missy Elliott and Jay-Z, it was taken back by black communities. However, to many African-Americans, this is a term that non-black people should simply never use. In 2017 writer and cultural critic Ta-Nehisi Coates was asked how he felt about white people using the "reclaimed" version of the *n*-word when reciting song lyrics, and he made the point that because our relationship to loaded words depends on our relationship to the oppression associated with them, not every reappropriated slur gets to belong to every group. Coates said, "The experience of being a hip-hop fan and not being able to use the word *ni**er* . . . will give you just a little peek into the world of what it means to be black. Because to be black is to walk through the world and watch people doing things that you cannot do."

herself, wishes the word *slut* would disappear. In 2017 the model and activist told *Playboy* magazine, "My goal this year is to . . . get *slut* out of the dictionary. I'm going to find out where [Webster's] headquarters are and tell my fans to come and protest with me, because the definition of a slut in the dictionary is a woman—a promiscuous woman."

Taking it upon ourselves to eradicate or redefine *slut* in everyday conversation will no doubt be more impact- ful than storming Webster's HQ. (As Deborah Cameron once said, "It's no good petitioning the King. . . . The struggle for meaning is a grassroots campaign.") But I appreciate Rose's intentions, and I'm wont to agree that in a culture that did not loathe women's sexual sovereignty with such gusto, the whole idea of a slut, and thus the word itself, would not resonate and therefore cease to exist. This sort of linguistic disappearing act has happened before. It's why terms like *old maid* and *spinster** seem passé—because, as of the twenty-first cen- tury, so does the idea of criticizing a woman for being over the age of forty and unmarried. Simply put, slurs go out of style at the same time the underlying belief in them does.

However, we all have our own relationships to differ-

* Another fun example of pejoration: a few hundred years ago, *spinster* was merely a job title for someone who spun yarn (which was usually a woman but not always). However, because women who spun to support themselves often did so because they didn't have husbands, the word became associated with the unwed. (It was once even a legal term for single women.) By the 1700s, *spinster* had stooped to describe women who were old, haggard, and bitter.

ent slurs, and mine to *slut* is a little different from Amber Rose's. Personally, I haven't used *slut* as a term of abuse or even thought of it that way for years. This is simply because I don't think there is such a thing as a slut in a negative sense given that I don't think there is such a thing as contemptible promiscuity in women. I still use the word *slut*—not a lot, but sparingly—and always in a positive, empowering, and sometimes ironic light, similar to the contexts Laurel Sutton observed with *ho* (e.g, "I had the sluttiest night ever, it was amazing"). Often my friends and I even use *slut* (and *whore*) in a nonsexual and gender-unspecific sense to describe one's fanatical enthusiasm for something (e.g., "Zack is such a whore for McDonald's fries" or "Amanda is the biggest wordslut I know"). Perhaps I stand by *slut* because it has that fun, plosive, single-syllable sound we all like so much. Perhaps it's because I personally haven't had too many traumatic experiences with the abusive usage of the word. Or perhaps it's simply because if you analyze a slur enough, eventually its sting is removed, like when you repeat a word over and over again until it loses all meaning and starts to sound weird. I'd like to believe that we can get to a point where female sexuality is never reprehensible. That way, anyone can identify as a slut if they want, knowing that little offense, if any, will result.

But words can't be positive all the time. In practice, insults are a linguistic need that will probably never go away (we're a critical bunch, us humans). So, when you do find yourself in need of an insult, to navigate the gender and sexism problem, here's another idea: instead of calling a woman a *cunt*, or a man a *motherfucker*, we could try to think of something gender neutral to say, choosing to focus on a person's behavior while verbally slighting them rather than their gender, which is more specific and effective anyway. For example, if someone of any gender does something conniving, we can call them a "shit-filled, two-faced sneak" or a "goddamn villainous crook," instead of a *bitch* or a *dick*—insults which happen to be more creative, scathing, and (importantly) relevant. If you want to get even more colorful about it, there are a few gender-neutral insults from foreign languages I quite enjoy. Perhaps try the Jamaican word *bumbaclot*, meaning "ass wipe," or the endearing (though hard to pronounce) Russian term *perhot' podzalupnaya*, meaning "pee hole dandruff."

The other positive thing we can do, says Zeisler, is to be mindful of the sexist terms we use around kids. Childhood and adolescence, after all, are when so many of these gendered stereotypes are solidified. "Take an active role in helping younger people break down what it is that they're really trying to say when they call someone a bitch or a slut or a pussy," Zeisler suggests, referencing an incident from 2008 when a college student called Hillary Clinton a bitch in front of her. "I asked him why he used that word in particular," Zeisler recalls. It turned out that this student didn't actually have strong, independently formed opinions about Hillary Clinton or what she should be called but instead had learned to refer to her as a bitch early in life because he grew up hearing his parents do it. Like the toddler who repeats "shit" over and over after hearing her mom let it slip out in the car, we absorb a hefty fraction of our unthinking gendered insult usage from our parents. In both positive and negative directions, future generations' offensive language habits are to some degree within our control. "There's so much in language that just becomes default," says Zeisler, "and so getting there early and challenging it is really crucial."

This isn't a matter of putting a moratorium on any given word out of political correctness or fear of offending. In fact, it's the opposite; it's a rebellion against the rules. By refusing to use words like *slut* and *pussy* as terms of abuse, you're rejecting the imbalanced standards that have been set for women's sexuality and men's machismo. It's a form of protest against the condemnation of women's sexual independence and men's refusal to act like chauvinist bruisers. And if enough people rebel, then everyone wins, because a society that's more equal is also one that's more relaxed, more compassionate, and less offended overall. If we're able to make like queers and dykes and own our insults, then the word *offense* itself will become obsolete.

Heightening our awareness of gendered insults gives us a better chance of becoming more conscious, more inclusive, and thus more accurate when we describe people's appearances and behaviors. That awareness, in turn, makes one think about how gender sneaks into other areas of our everyday speech. If we're going to analyze what the word *slut* really means, where it comes from, and why we say it, the next natural step is to ask the same questions about the rest of the gendered words we habitually use without thinking, like *woman*, *man*, *female*, *male*, *guy*, *girl*, *she*, *he*, etc. Why do gender and sex, as opposed to any other identifying qualities, play such a fundamental role in how we talk about people? Why is singling out a person's gender through language so important to us?

I figured there had to be a story there. And, oh my word, there was . . .

wait ... what does the word *woman* mean anyway?

plus other questions of sex, gender, and the language behind them

2

There was once a gifted rocket scientist named Yvonne Brill. Born in Winnipeg, Canada, Brill spent her prodigious three-decade career dreaming up dazzling new ways for NASA to send starships and satellites into the great beyond. Brill attended the University of Manitoba, though she was not allowed to study engineering due to the fact that she possessed a vulva. (Unclear whether or not the admissions office personally confirmed her vulva, but because of the little *f* on her birth certificate, they evidently wagered a guess and stamped "Nope, no engineering for you, dear" on her transcript.) She wasn't deterred. Brill majored in chemistry and mathematics instead, and years later, she developed a rocket engine so efficient and reliable that it became standard throughout the industry. If you've ever watched the local news, looked up the weather, or used a GPS, you have Dr. Brill to thank.

When Brill died in 2013 at the age of eighty-eight, the world of aerospace engineering mourned her deeply, and a couple days later, the *New York Times* ran an obituary that started a little something like this:

> She made a mean beef stroganoff, followed her husband from job to job and took eight years off from work to raise three children. "The world's best mom," her son Matthew said.
>
> But Yvonne Brill, who died on Wednesday at 88 in Princeton, N.J., was also a brilliant rocket scientist . . .

And everyone was really, really confused.

Yvonne Brill spent decades launching missions to the moon and to Mars. In 2011 President Obama awarded her the National Medal of Technology and Innovation. But damn, that stroganoff. And lest we forget those eight years she took off to nurture her offspring (which didn't actually happen; she just went part-time). In the eyes of the *Times*, however, those trappings of traditional femininity not only defined Brill more than her contributions to the cosmos, they were—as the "but" at the start of their second paragraph implies—in direct contradiction.

The *Times* didn't get away with their sexist aspersion of Brill's life. They hastily struck the stroganoff reference after a veritable shitstorm of criticism echoed throughout the press, lamenting the obit's emphasis on Brill's stereotypical embodiment of *womanness* (the food, the babies) rather than her intergalactic reputation. As book critic Edward Champion tweeted that week, the paper's death notice of Mahatma Gandhi likely would not have read, "[He] made a great frittata, ironed some shirts, and took eight years off to catch up on Hardy Boys books."

I came across the problematic opening of Brill's obit in college and it instantly piqued my interest, because it posed the challenging question: At the end of the day (or at the end of a life, as it were), what does the word *woman* truly represent? That is, when English speakers label someone a woman, what image do we intend to put in a listener's mind? Is a woman defined by certain gender roles (a devoted wife and nurturing cook)? Is womanness classified by presentation (long hair, makeup, dresses)? Is it the body that potentially allows childbearing, the vulva that excluded Brill from U of M's engineering program? Or is that instead what we mean when we say *female*? Also, why are some people offended by explicitly gendering an accomplished professional who happens to be a woman, like Yvonne Brill—calling her "a *woman* scientist," as opposed to just "a scientist"—while others aren't? Perhaps *woman* is becoming one of those words that means something different to everyone. But if that is indeed the case, how do we figure out how to use it?

Some people argue that if we want gender equality, then we should avoid using the word *woman* in public whenever possible. From their perspective, it's sexist to call out a woman's gender in contexts where the same wouldn't be done for a man. You may have heard one or two high-achieving women tell an interviewer, "I don't want to be known as a *woman* such-and-such, I just want to be known as that thing, no qualifiers." In 1996 television director Gloria Muzio said: "It's always been important to me and crucial to be thought of as a good director, not as a good *woman* director, but unfortunately, I've been singled out at times as a woman."

Perhaps the biggest critic of adding women's genders to their accomplishments is UC Berkeley scholar Robin Lakoff. Often considered the founding parent of the study of gender and language, Lakoff wrote an explosively influential book in 1975 called *Language and Woman's Place*, which sparked great debate about the role language plays in creating gender stereotypes. To say "woman scientist," "woman president," or "woman doctor" implies that a woman filling these roles is "in some way unnatural," Lakoff once told the *New York Times*. What these gendered qualifiers do is suggest that it is an exception for women to have well-regarded professions, and that messaging can creep into our real-life decision-making. Lakoff continued: "Every time we say 'woman president,' we reinforce the view that only a man can be commander in chief [and] symbolize the US (which is metonymically Uncle Sam and not Aunt Samantha, after all), and make it harder to conceive of, and hence vote for, a woman in that role."

Not everyone agrees that calling attention to a woman's gender is bad, even in contexts where you wouldn't do so for a man. The way some folks see it, because it's still harder for women to succeed in science, medicine, and politics, highlighting their gender helps make women in these fields more visible. It's seen as an inspiration.

Others argue that whether you call someone like Dr. Brill an engineer or a *woman* engineer, it won't make much of a difference in how people conceive of engineers in general. Linguistic studies show that many gender-neutral job titles (*cardiologist, construction worker*) are still usually interpreted as men's jobs, no matter what words you use to describe them. (Equally, titles like *housekeeper* and *babysitter* are interpreted as women's jobs, even though the words themselves don't make any reference to gender.) Furthermore, when new words that are meant to be gender-inclusive are introduced to the lexicon (*chairperson* instead of *chairman, business-person* versus *businessman, firefighter* versus *fireman*), they often wind up becoming another feminine term—an outlier in a world where *man* is still the default. There will

wordslut

always be people who continue to call a businessperson a *businessman* and will only switch to the gender-inclusive term when the subject is female—a sign that adjusting one's language in the right direction doesn't necessarily cause one's unconscious thinking to follow.

Another important branch of the "to gender or not to gender" debate is whether to call someone a woman or a female. The dispute has stirred up real controversy. In 2015, after Hillary Clinton announced the start of her presidential campaign, political pundits went berserk over whether she should (if elected) go by the term "woman president" or "female president."

This semantic bickering was justifiable, even if most of those reporters didn't understand exactly why: in practical usage, *woman* and *female* are not, in fact, interchangeable. Our Oxford linguist Deborah Cameron found proof of this in the British National Corpus (a comprehensive database containing over one hundred million written and spoken English words collected from a wide variety of sources. The corpus is meant to serve as a representative sample of late-twentieth-century British English). After scanning the database, Cameron found that when people use *female* as a noun, as opposed to *woman*, it's often in explicitly negative contexts. For example:

1. **My poor Clemence was as helpless a female as you'd find in a long day's march.**

2. "Stupid, crazy female" was all he said as he set about bandaging it.
3. A call yesterday involved giving the chatty female at the other end one's address.

These examples all involve a speaker passing derogatory judgment on the subject. And though their statements would still be insulting if you swapped in the word *woman*, they would be, as Cameron says, "less unequivocally contemptuous." The corpus data also showed that the noun form of *female* is almost never used in a positive context. You wouldn't hear someone say, "My best friend is the kindest, most generous female I have ever met."

Why, when aiming to make a disparaging comment about a woman, do speakers often choose to use the word *female*? Cameron postulates that it might have something to do with the desire to point out that women are flawed by biological design. The implication is that *female*, a scientific term used to describe bodies throughout the animal kingdom, refers to one's sex (one's genitalia, chromosomes, gonads, and other reproductive body parts). Meanwhile, *woman*, a term only used to describe humans, refers to gender, a culturally invented and much more complex concept (which we'll attempt to define in a bit). By choosing to label someone a "stupid, crazy *female*," it suggests that the subject's intellectual flaws are connected to her vulva, XX chromosomes,

wait . . . what does the word woman mean anyway?

wordslut

uterus, etc., as if the very sex classification of her body is responsible for these negative traits.

The gender versus sex question is one of the most critical sides of the *woman* vs. *female* semantic debate: Is the word *woman* what we should use to describe gender, which refers to something cultural and conceptual, while *female* is what we should use to describe sex, which refers to something of the body? Why is sex versus gender an important concept to articulate in the first place? And furthermore, why are the words we currently have to describe it so unclear?

To find out a word's "true" meaning, our first step is usually to look up the official definition. But even the dictionary doesn't offer a clear solution to the sex-gender puzzle. As of the time I'm writing this, the world's four most referenced dictionaries (the *Collins Dictionary, Merriam-Webster, Dictionary.com*, and the *Oxford English Dictionary*) all define the word *woman* as an adult human female. This definition implies that to be a woman and to be a female are necessarily connected. So what is a female, then? These dictionaries all define *female* as "of the sex that produces ova and bears offspring" (or some slight variation of this). From there, one can make the connection that, according to the dictionary, in order to be a woman one must be an adult who produces ova and offspring. The definition is a bodily one. (Similarly, these dictionaries all define *man* as an adult male person, though Merriam-Webster's top *man* entry simply reads "an individual human"—a glaring reflection of that pervasive default maleness concept.)

Keep paging through definitions for *woman* and you'll find secondary entries reading "a female servant or domestic help" and "a wife, mistress, or girlfriend." These labels have nothing at all to do with body parts—they describe culturally invented roles and relationships, and they certainly don't apply to every woman.

Ultimately, this mishmash of definitions scrambles the cultural and bodily aspects of gender and sex, making the definition of *woman* incredibly muddy.

The confusion isn't dictionary makers' fault. The job of a dictionary writer is not to conclusively solve our most confounding language conundrums; instead, it's to reflect "general usage," or how most English speakers use and understand a word at the time of the dictionary's writing, even if it's murky or politically incorrect. Where gender is concerned, however, dictionary definitions become inherently political. And they can have real legislative consequences. Consider one case from 2002, where the Kansas Supreme Court nullified the marriage of a transgender woman and her recently deceased husband, maintaining that, according to the dictionary, "The words *sex*, *male*, and *female* in everyday understanding do not encompass transsexuals." Using the dictionary as dogma, the court classified the bereaved wife as a man involved in a then-illegal same-sex marriage, and she was forbidden from inheriting her husband's estate.

Events like this are partially why a group of boycotters on Twitter petitioned the *Collins Dictionary* in 2017 to change the definition of *woman* to be more inclusive and not so dependent on body parts. While protesting a staff of nerdy, underpaid lexicographers is not the most effective way to enact social change, it is true that as a society, treating dictionary definitions as fixed, unbiased facts is a mistake. Word meanings and cultural beliefs go hand in hand, and they are both changing all the time.

The problem those *Collins Dictionary* boycotters were attempting to address was a real one: If a woman is a female and a female is someone with ova and offspring, then what is a woman who, say, was born without ova, or had to get them removed due to some medical condition? What is an intersex* woman, who maybe has a vagina and XY chromosomes but also testes? And is it really right that in 2002 the court got to decide whether or not a transgender widow earned the label of woman, when their evidence for doing so was a dictionary entry that is no arbiter of truth but rather a mirror of what everyday people all personally believed at the time?

Again, I ask, what does the word *woman* mean, really?

---

* *Intersex* is a term that generally refers to a number of conditions in which a person is born with reproductive or sexual anatomy that doesn't quite fit our traditional definition of female or male. To be born intersex is not as rare as people think. According to research conducted in 2000, the total percentage of people whose bodies differ from standard male or female (which could mean variations in chromosomes, hormones, gonads, or genitals) is 1.7 percent. That's approximately the same percentage of natural redheads in the United States.

The sex versus gender concept is befuddling in part because of the etymology of the word *gender* itself. Believe it or not, *gender* didn't enter the mainstream English lexicon until the late twentieth century. According to the Corpus of Historical American English, which contains a massive four hundred million words from the 1810s to the 2000s, most people didn't start using the word *gender* to describe human beings until the 1980s. That's when its conversational frequency raised from just one occurrence per million words to five occurrences per million. Until the late fifteenth century, *gender* was only ever used to describe grammatical categories, like masculine and feminine nouns. Never people. The *Oxford English Dictionary*'s first recorded usage of *gender* to describe humans doesn't appear until 1474. But at that time, the word was just a synonym for *sex*—the state of being "male or female"—which is how it would be understood for the next five hundred years. It's possible that people still confuse the bodily sense of masculinity and femininity (now understood as *sex*) and the cultural or identity part of it (*gender*) because these words have been used interchangeably for half a millennium. No one ever posed a semantic distinction between sex and gender until the 1960s, when folks began to realize that our bodies and social behaviors might not be intrinsically linked.

The first people to put the difference between sex and gender on our mainstream cultural radar were second-wave feminist activists in the mid-twentieth century. These second-wavers (whose goals included things like equal pay and reproductive rights) found it politically helpful to distinguish what they saw as self-evident biological sex from all of the cultural expectations that get imposed on people based on their sex. Activists wanted to make the statement that women weren't inherently suited to the sorts of lives most of them were cornered into leading at the time. Their goal was to invalidate the prevailing thought that women were "naturally" inclined toward cooking, sewing, and curtsying, as opposed to more stereotypically masculine proclivities, like wearing suits and running the world.

Second-wave feminists were highly vocal about the sex-gender distinction, but they technically weren't the first to name it. A few decades before their movement took hold, gender as a societal construct was an obscure academic concept.* In 1945 the *Oxford English Dictionary* defined

---

* This isn't to say feminists weren't thinking about the differences between sex and gender before they had distinct labels to describe them. Simone de Beauvoir's famous 1949 quote, "One is not born, but rather

gender as "the state of being male or female as expressed by social or cultural distinctions and differences, rather than biological ones." The definition's example sentence came from an academic psychology article published around that time and reads, "In the grade school years, too, gender (which is the socialised obverse of sex) is a fixed line of demarcation, the qualifying terms being 'feminine' and 'masculine.'"

It was also social scientists who first connected the word *gender* to internal identity (the gut feeling of who you think you are), as opposed to the culturally learned behavior part (the makeup, the cooking, the deferential tone of voice). The identity-based definition of gender first came up in the 1950s among psychiatrists in writings pertaining to the clinical treatment of what they labeled "transexuals" and "hermaphrodites," whom we would now call transgender and intersex folks.

One such psychiatrist was Robert Stoller, who conducted his research in the 1950s at UCLA's Gender Identity Clinic. Stoller believed there was a biological basis for what he termed "core gender identity," defined as "an innate sense of being male or female which is normally fixed by the second year of life." He also believed nurture was heavily involved. A student of Freud, Stoller bought into the (now discredited) idea that a person's sexual desires, especially what were known as "perversions"

becomes, a woman," implies a clear understanding of the culture versus body discrepancy, even though nowhere in it does the word *gender* appear.

wordslut

(homosexuality, transvestism, sadomasochism), developed in direct response to traumatic early life events that "threatened" one's core gender identity.

Since Stoller's time, curiosity and examination of human gender have vastly increased, but the definition of the word has not simplified. Instead, it has only gotten even more complex, even for psychologists and linguists. This isn't a unique phenomenon—word meanings inevitably evolve and expand over time.* Just as we can't expect any given culture to stay the same forever, we can't expect its words to go unchanged either.

Frustrating as it may be, there is ultimately not one simple definition of the word *gender* or *man* or *woman*. Some use *gender* to refer to a set of culturally learned behaviors, or a social status imposed upon them as a result of their sex. Others use it to mean an inherent sense of identity linked to their instinct or brain. Some use it to mean both. Deborah Cameron defines *gender* as "an extraordinarily intricate and multilayered phenomenon—unstable, contested, intimately bound up with other social divisions." Her colleague Sally McConnell-Ginet, a linguist at Cornell, calls it "[a] complex system of cognitive, symbolic, behavioral, political, and social phenomena mediated by sorting of people according to their sex." According to McConnell-Ginet, the significance and content of being any given gender

---

* Back in Chaucer's day, the word *girl* meant a child of any sex. In Old English, *pretty* meant crafting or cunning. In Middle English, *dinner* literally meant breakfast.

can vary among cultures, individuals, life stages, even momentary situations. Translation: it is damn complicated.

And all the while, some people still use the word *gender* when what they really want to talk about is *sex*—like when pregnant parents reveal the "gender" of their unborn babies. (My theory is that some English speakers continue to do this simply because prudish Westerners are too afraid to say the word *sex* out loud.) Two people could be using the same word, *gender*, in a single conversation but could be talking about any number of completely different things.

If gender isn't something that comes fully formed at birth, where exactly do each of our genders come from then? This might not seem like a language question, but some philosophers theorize that gender is actually constructed *through* language itself. Their idea is that people don't talk the way they do as a result of the gender they already have; they don't simply reflect that gender through words (say, by calling yourself a woman because you know you're a woman or using "feminine" curse words like *gosh darnit* instead of *goddamnit* because you've been socialized to be polite). Instead, it's just the opposite: people have the genders that they do *because* of the way they talk and the feedback they receive from that talk. Language brings gender to life.

The idea here is that we are all in a constant ongoing process of using language to construct our genders. This notion was first articulated in the 1990s by a gender theorist at UC Berkeley named Judith Butler. She came up with a theory called *gender performativity*, which essentially says that gender isn't something you *are*, it's something you *do*. As far as Butler is concerned, humans don't exist until we do things that bring us into being; that is, who a person is and what a person does come to exist "simultaneously," as if, at the very same time that you learn about and engage in social practices, you—and your gender identity—emerge.

So the words we use don't only reflect who we are, they actively *create* who we are. How? One big way this happens is by people self-identifying their genders through certain labels, pronouns, and terms of address. It is beyond the scope of this book to present a glossary of terms for every gender and sexual identity that exists, from *cisgender* to *transgender* to *graygender* to *pansexual* to *asexual*, and beyond. This vocabulary is ever-evolving. For some speakers it may feel hard to keep up, but it's important to understand that these labels aren't surfacing just because it's suddenly trendy to have an identity that will perplex and/or piss off all our great-aunts and -uncles at Thanksgiving.* Sociolinguists agree the creation of these different categories is connected to a deeper human desire to typologize species—

---

* Though I have heard of a gender identity called a *genderfuck*, which is defined by one who presents clashing or incongruous gender signals. A genderfuck (sometimes called a *genderpunk*) might wear makeup but also have a beard and might use a variety of different pronouns interchangeably (sometimes going by *she*, sometimes by *he*, sometimes by *they*). I imagine such an identity would make most of our great-uncles rather disoriented, which, as I take it, is part of the point.

to identify groups of living things, sort them, and try to figure out what their relationship is to one another. It's a form of taxonomy: we create these labels to help make sense of the world around us and ourselves.

This need to typologize different genders and sexualities in order to understand them better is hardly new. In nineteenth-century Germany, there was a pretty robust research institute called the Scientific-Humanitarian Committee (now recognized as the first-ever LGBTQ+ rights organization) dedicated to this exact kind of classification. The group was founded by Magnus Hirschfeld, a Jewish physician and researcher of human sexuality living in Berlin. Known as the "Einstein of Sex," Hirschfeld was one of the first Western scientists to recognize a sex and gender spectrum—as opposed to the binary divisions of male and female, man and woman— and he developed a system of categories to describe different points along this continuum. Hirschfeld's groupings accounted for sixty-four possible types of sexualities and genders, ranging from masculine heterosexual males to feminine homosexual males to *transvestit*, a term he coined in 1910 to describe people who we would now call transgender. In Hirschfeld's mind, there existed a singular, accurate, biology-supported definition for every one of these sex and gender labels, just as there exists a singular, accurate, biology-supported definition for each type of invertebrate, from annelids to cnidarians.

In the following decades, scientists would come to realize that human gender and sexuality can't be typologized or explained on a purely biological basis: most human phenomena—from intelligence to addiction—are, to some extent, a combination of both nature *and* nurture. Still, Hirschfeld's contributions were substantial, and his compulsion to find names and natural bases for these seemingly inexplicable personal identities was logical. He thought that if he could come up with a scientific explanation for nonnormative genders and sexualities, put a label on them, and prove they weren't moral failings, then that would change the political situation for so many people. In Hirshfield's time (and throughout the nineteenth and twentieth centuries), nonnormative gender and sexual identities were punishable by law. This was true not only in Germany but in most other Western countries as well, including the United States. Hirschfeld and his colleagues figured if they could scientifically validate what were seen as "deviant" identities, then maybe the laws would change.

Fortunately, today, you can no longer be arrested—in most English-speaking places, at least—for who you want to sleep with or what gender you are (though hate crimes are certainly still prevalent). But there's still an intense drive to come up with language to describe these different identities. We still crave labels. Linguists say that this has everything to do with the power of words to legitimize experiences, as if an idea only becomes valid once it's christened with a title. "It's clearly empowering for people to discover that they're not the only ones having an experience and that the experience can be named," explains UCSB gender and language scholar Lal Zimman. Not everyone is empowered by categorization, and it is possible that one day nonnormative genders and sexualities will become so accepted that this spectrum of labels won't seem necessary. But in the meantime, labels offer validation to many folks who previously felt isolated and unheard.

As of the mid-2010s, the term *nonbinary* has started making its way into everyday vocabularies. In 2018 California became the first state to offer nonbinary as a third category on official birth certificates, so that folks who are intersex and/or gender-nonconforming can have the option of legally changing their identification later in life. A year earlier, Oregon became the first state to allow a nonbinary "X" gender symbol on driver's licenses. As attitudes about gender slowly continue to change, so will our language.

English speakers can't consider themselves particularly creative or progressive in the nonnormative gender department, though. That's because we are not the first to describe the gender spectrum—not by a long shot. On every continent, since the beginning of civilization, dozens of thriving cultures have recognized and offered words to describe three or four, sometimes five genders. Just as linguist Sally McConnell-Ginet mentioned in her definition, gender differs not only from person to person but also between entire cultures, depending on how certain bodies and behaviors are interpreted.

In India, *hijras* are folks who are considered neither

wordslut

men nor women. Someone from the United States might describe *hijras* as transgender women who were assigned male at birth (AMAB).* But in Indian culture, they are a totally separate third gender. Accordingly, *hijras* have special gender roles in society, serving as mythical figures who don't participate in reproduction, giving them power to bless or curse others' fertility.

The Buginese people of Indonesia recognize five genders: women, men, *calalai*, *calabai*, and *bissu*. *Calalai* are assigned female at birth (AFAB) and embody a masculine gender identity; *calabai* are AMAB and embody a feminine gender identity. *Bissu* are "transcendent gender," meaning they encompass all of these identities, serving key roles in Buginese traditions, and are sometimes equated with priests.

In the Native American Zuni tribe, a third gender called *lhamana*—also described as mixed-gender or Two-Spirit—encompasses people who live as both men and women simultaneously. Two-Spirits are AMAB but wear a mixture of men's and women's clothing and mostly perform traditional women's work, like pottery and cooking. One of the most famous Two-Spirits was a figure named We'wha, who served as the Zuni ambas-

---

* ICYMI: A more accepted way to refer to a person's physiology outside of their gender is not to say "biologically female" or "biologically male," but instead to say AFAB or AMAB, which stand for "assigned female at birth" and "assigned male at birth." The idea is that the sex of a person is not necessarily a "biological fact" but is instead determined by a doctor's brief evaluation of a baby's genitalia without taking into consideration any of their other sex characteristics (and certainly not their gender identity—not that a newborn baby has one yet). Also, while we're talking abbreviations, ICYMI stands for "in case you missed it." ICYMI.

sador to the United States in the late 1800s. We'wha spent six months in Washington, DC, where she was reportedly beloved by the establishment. Those white government bros had no idea We'wha wasn't a "woman" by their standards; as far as they could tell, that word fit her. But back among the Zunis, We'wha went by a totally different label.

More fascinating still, gender isn't the only identity that falls along a spectrum: there are even cultural differences between how *female* and *male* in the sex/body sense are defined. In the Dominican Republic, there happens to be a high incidence of a rare genetic intersex condition called 5-ARD. Babies with 5-ARD are born with what appear to be female genitalia, but at puberty, their bodies—from their faces to their nether regions—start to masculinize, and by adulthood, they look like hairy, barrel-chested men. In Dominican culture, people with 5-ARD are labeled *guevedoces*, which literally means "penis at twelve." In this community, people with 5-ARD are raised as girls, but after puberty, they are considered men for the rest of their lives, and they often take on new, masculine names. For the Dominican Republic, people with 5-ARD are just "girls" whose bodies and minds suddenly become "boys."

Ten thousand miles away, in Papua New Guinea, there are also noticeably high numbers of 5-ARD. But unlike the *guevedoces*, these people are not recognized as first a girl and then a boy; instead, they are seen as an entirely different sex, a third sex, both before and after puberty. They are labeled *turnim-man* and are acknowledged by the community as such, which informs their lifelong identities. So even though these folks have the same bodies as the Dominican *guevedoces*—the same XY chromosomes, the same ambiguous genitalia—based on the cultural perceptions in Papua New Guinea, they are called by a different name.

In English, we are constantly coming up with new names to describe different pockets of the sex and gender spectrum. We find ourselves in a cultural moment where how we think about gender, and human sociology in general, is being driven by what Zimman calls "self-definition." Thanks to things like the internet, personal brands, and other modern ideas about individualism, each of us gets to define who we are to the world on our own terms, and we can tweak those definitions over the course of our lives. We're not annelids or anthropoids, after all; we're human beings with complex thoughts and experiences that are in constant evolution. Almost nothing about our identities can be defined on such rigid terms—gender included. If you're a woman, you're a person who self-identifies as a woman, no matter what your body, mannerisms, or style of dress look like. "That actually bypasses the traditional idea that women see themselves as women because they liked to play with dolls when they were little and that men see themselves as men because they liked to play sports," says Zimman. These props don't have to be what defines our gender anymore. "Instead," he says, "it's just this very individualized, emotional, visceral feeling of who do I think I am."

If there are no hard-and-fast definitions of the words *woman*, *female*, *man*, or *male*, then how do we know when to use them? There is, I'm afraid, no single rule we can all follow here either—in every case, the context and intent of the conversation will factor in. I have my own personal language preferences. For example, if someone wants to call me a "woman writer" or a "female writer," that's chill, especially since I write a lot about things that pertain specifically to women. But there are other gendered terms that make me cringe. I happen not to enjoy when people call me *ma'am*,* which makes me feel drab and old (something women are not supposed to be in our culture), though I hate being called *miss*, too, which sounds belittling. Men are so lucky they just get to be called *sir* no matter their age or marital status.

Several years ago I also became conscious of how English speakers use *you guys*. Often used as an address term for folks of any gender, *guys* is casual and friendly, and it solves a grammatical hiccup, since English lacks a second-person plural pronoun. Many speakers genuinely believe *guys* has become gender neutral. However,

---

* *Ma'am* is not considered so objectionable by all English speakers. In British English, the term is considered so formal and deferent that one would only use it for nobility, never an everyday person. My friends in the American South also by and large find *ma'am* to be a polite and expected courtesy, and would use it to address women of any age or marital status, from teachers and mothers-in-law to young girls. The rules of linguistic politeness differ significantly from language to language and culture to culture. (I personally still hate *ma'am*, though.)

scholars agree that *guys* is just another masculine generic in cozier clothing. There'd be no chance of *you gals* earning the same lexical love, and people who actively avoid gender-biased words like *ma'am* often still use *guys*, as if it were any less gendered. Before the 1980s, *guys* was only ever used to describe men, and once it evolved to encompass women, many sociolinguists were shocked. Steven J. Clancy, a Harvard linguist, once said of the phrase: "Contrary to everything we might expect because of the pressures of 'politically correct' putative language reforms, a new generic noun is developing right before our eyes." The trouble with *you guys* is ultimately why *y'all* has become my second-person plural of choice, as I mentioned fifty or so pages ago.

But not everyone is bothered by the same gendered words. Not to mention it would be just plain awkward to correct some polite stranger when they call me *miss* or group me in with *you guys*. But what I can say with some confidence is that in general practice, it's a lovely idea to address people, especially people we don't know, in a way that doesn't assume this deeply complex thing that is their gender, particularly when it isn't relevant to the situation at hand. This can be easily done by swapping in gender-neutral terms like *folks* instead of *guys* or *ladies*, or just leaving out the gendered word entirely—a simple "Excuse me," instead of "Excuse me, *ma'am*," will usually do the trick just fine.

Another useful thing we can do to make our language more inclusive, especially when gender *is* pertinent to the conversation, is to be much more specific with our word choices. Say we're talking about reproductive health. Instead of saying something like "women need access to cervical cancer screenings," we can get more specific and say, "people with cervixes need access to cervical cancer screenings." This language is taboo, Zimman says, because it's not participating in a euphemizing of sex. But it's an example of how speaking in an inclusive way is also more accurate, especially since not all women have cervixes; not all people with cervixes are women; having a cervix doesn't make you a woman, it just makes you a person with a cervix; and also "people with cervixes" is just a cuter marketing phrase anyway.

Will making these slight linguistic tweaks realistically push people's attitudes toward gender and sex in a more accepting direction? Can forcing someone to say "hi, folks" instead of "hi, guys," or to call Yvonne Brill an "engineer" instead of a "woman engineer" really change their perspective of gender at large?

This, linguists admit, is empirically hard to measure. However, what we know is that even if changing our own language won't necessarily change our thinking, the language we hear from other people can. For example, imagine if it became the policy at a restaurant to cease addressing people as "ladies" and "gentlemen" or "Mrs. So-and-So" and "Mr. So-and-So" but instead to use the gender-neutral terms *guests* and *Mx.** There

*This is a non–gender-specific honorific that was coined in the 1970s and officially added to Merriam-Webster's dictionary in September 2017.

could be a server at this restaurant who is totally against the rule. But the manager makes them follow it with the restaurant's patrons, including young kids, who then hear this language, and that could very well have an impact on them even if it didn't change the speaker's mind.

There are places around the world where such policies have worked. In 2017 Vice documented two kindergarteners in Sweden who were AMAB but have gender-neutral names, long hair, and are allowed to play with whatever toys they like, from dinosaurs to nail polish, without gender associations. In Sweden, enforcing gender stereotypes in schools has actually been illegal since 1998. Instead, the government funds gender-neutral kindergartens, where you'll find teachers saying "friends" instead of "boys" and "girls"; lessons are taught using gender-neutral mediums, like nature and modeling clay; toy animals replace baby dolls; and characters in books are pictured defying traditional gender roles (female pirates; lesbian queens ruling a kingdom; Batman wearing a baby in a sling around his torso). An obituary of a woman rocket scientist in Sweden would, no doubt, never open with "she followed her husband around from job to job."

That Yvonne Brill obituary, by the way, was penned by the *New York Times*'s obit columnist at the time, who was, to no one's surprise, a dude. The journalism business, much like most formal industries involving language, has been helmed by men since the beginning of modern English. But what does language sound like when men aren't around to influence it? Lucky for us, sociolinguists have studied how our words change when women are both the speakers and the listeners. Experts have entered those precious spaces—the enclaves of our apartments, the dugouts of our softball leagues—where women manage to ephemerally escape the perspectives and expectations of a society run by bros. And what they've found is very cool indeed.

"mm-hmm, girl, you're right"

how women talk to each other when dudes aren't around

In 1922 Professor Otto Jespersen published his tour de force, a book called *Language*. At the time of its release, *Language* was the single most exhaustive account of the derivation and development of human speech to date. Then sixty-two years old, Jespersen was a linguist at Denmark's University of Copenhagen whose specialties included syntax, the study of sentence structures, and early language development. His book was exhaustive—*Language* covered sounds, words, grammar, the origin of speech (these are real chapter titles). There was even a chapter called "The Woman."

Jespersen's "The Woman" chapter addressed women's everyday speech habits and how those habits differ from men's. It was his interpretation of "girl talk." It's reasonable to think of *Language* and "The Woman" like a big, prestigious medical textbook that reserved just one section, about two-thirds of the way through, for "women's" health. As if to say, well, there are bodies and then there are *lady* bodies, which are at once an entirely different subject and also only worth dedicating about 10.4 percent of our attention to (the precise quotient of Jespersen's fleshy 448-page tome occupied by "The Woman"). This medical textbook analogy is no hypothetical, by the way; studies of gender bias in med school literature from all over the world have found that even in seemingly objective educational materials, male bodies—like male speech patterns—are typically considered the norm and that symptoms more often found in women are given less attention or ignored altogether. Just look at heart disease, which was the number one cause of death among American women as of 2015 (that's more than all cancers combined). Women make up more than half of total heart disease fatalities, yet men are still more likely to be diagnosed. Why? Because female subjects are mostly absent from medical textbooks and papers, many doctors simply don't know how to recognize or treat heart disease in women, whose symptoms usually show up differently than men's (like nausea and neck discomfort as opposed to chest pain).

So Jespersen's book was very much like that, but for language. Louise O. Vasvári, language professor at NYU, has less-than-favorable thoughts about his "The Woman" chapter. "He had no chapter called 'men' or even 'young men' or 'old men' or any kind of minority men," she laments. "Because *Language* was man's language, of course, and then you have this one chapter, saying, oh, how interesting, how strange, these women and their language."

Drawing from his own anecdotal observations of women, not empirical studies, plus a hodgepodge of popular texts (Shakespearean plays, magazine articles, anonymous French proverbs), Jespersen decrees that the way women talk is curiously inferior—less masterful, less effective—to that of men. His conclusions include gems like, "Women more often than men break off without finishing their sentences, because they start talking without having thought out what they are going to say," "The vocabulary of a woman as a rule is much less extensive than that of a man," and "The highest linguistic genius and the lowest degree of linguistic imbecility are very rarely found among women. The great orators, the most famous literary artists, have been men."

"Ridiculous," Vasvári responds dryly, ninety-five years later. "Totally ridiculous."

But Jespersen, as it turns out, was only partially ridiculous. What was definitely ridiculous was the man's

wordslut

lack of any sort of data to support statements like, "Men take greater interest in [words'] acoustic properties. . . . [A man] chews the cud to make sure of the taste of words . . . thus preparing himself for the appropriate use of the fittest noun or adjective." (Yes, you just read the word *cud*, which I think is safe to place on the list of the grossest English words, next to *moist*, *panties*, and *pustule*.)

But what was not so ridiculous at all was that Otto Jespersen was one of the first linguists to write about the idea that how people talk, and how our speech is perceived, might have something to do with whether a person is a man or a woman (or somewhere else along the spectrum, as we'd come to discover), and how those gender roles are perceived.

One of the most commonly misunderstood speech styles in the English language is how women communicate among themselves—how they use language when there are no men in the conversation. Thoughts about "girl talk," as these exchanges are often labeled, are generally informed by the culture-wide assumptions that women are more emotional, less sure of themselves, and naturally inclined to talk about so-called frivolous topics, like lip gloss and the Kardashians. "Girl talk," suggests that when women converse with one another it's inherently featherbrained and precious. Not to mention the implication that women all talk to each other in private the same way. When Supreme Court justices Ruth Bader Ginsburg and Sonia Sotomayor run into each other in the bathroom between hearings, do their sink-side exchanges also count as "girl talk?"

Imperfect label or not, I do believe most women can sense that there's something special about the way women communicate among other women (and not "inferior" special like Otto Jespersen believed). Growing up in a culture with so many rigid standards and expectations for feminine behavior, the ways in which women are "supposed" to talk out in the world—in meetings, in line at the grocery store—are in part a curated performance. *Don't ask too many questions or you'll sound unassertive; don't say anything negative about a child or you'll sound like a nonmaternal sociopath; don't make too many allusions to* The Bachelor *or you'll sound basic.* No matter your sexuality or gender presentation, anyone who has ever been female, either in birth assignment or identity, is unavoidably still dragooned into following some patriarchal convention of feminine speech.

So how do women speak when they're in the exclusive company of other women? What does woman-on-woman conversation sound like, according to data from linguists? Is it different in any meaningful capacity from how men talk with other men? And what can all that teach us about femininity itself?

Since Otto Jespersen's time, linguists have found some answers to these questions. One of the foremost scholars of "girl talk" is Jennifer Coates, a linguist at the University of Roehampton in Britain. Coates, now in her seventies,

wordslut

has more than three decades of expertise in the field of gender and conversational style; and though she would never use the phrase "girl talk," her work provides plenty of support for the idea that women often communicate differently when surrounded solely by other women. Over the decades, Coates and her peers have carefully examined the speech styles of many different all-women and all-men groups—these are called *genderlects*. They've looked at various ages, races, cultures, sexualities, and socioeconomic classes, and while there is undoubtedly variation based on these factors, not to mention the context of the conversations (speech usually varies from the brunch table to the boardroom), one observation has remained rather constant: while men's speech style can be categorized as "competitive," women's is "cooperative."

Analyze a few hundred transcripts of dude-on-dude chatter and you'll usually find a dominant speaker who holds the floor, and a subordinate waiting for his turn. It's a vertical structure. But with women, the conversation is frequently much more horizontal and malleable; everyone is an equal player. While men tend to view conversation as an arena for establishing hierarchies and expressing individual achievement, women's goals are typically to support the other speakers and emphasize solidarity. Thus, women progressively build on what one another says.

There are lots of misconceptions about men's and women's speech styles, especially when it comes to the topics they talk about. You may have heard the banality that women talk about "people," whereas men talk about "ideas." This stereotype is the linguistic analogue of assuming that when women get together, all they do is have pillow fights, paint their nails, and talk about their celebrity crushes. Nonetheless, some of the most discerning figures in media still buy into it. In 2016 writer Andrea Wulf won the Royal Society Insight Investment Science Book prize for a biography of the Prussian naturalist Alexander von Humboldt, and in response, a male journalist from the *Guardian* theorized that the reason women have started winning more science book awards is not that more women are writing books about science but that "female science writers" are "more likely to focus on people, while their male counterparts are more likely to address a problem, a mystery, or an underexplored scientific field." It's men that make the real discoveries, he implies—women are just there to make their stories all warm and snuggly.

The way Jennifer Coates sees it, it's often true that women's topics of conversation center on people and feelings, while men tend to steer in the direction of things and events—sports,* gadgets, current affairs. (This

* One of my greatest cultural pet peeves is the belief that watching, playing, and talking about sports are more prestigious and valuable than taking an interest in beauty or fashion. I once worked at a beauty magazine where most of the staff was female but several of the higher-ups were men. It was hard not to notice how tirelessly these guys worked to assert their manliness by making sports references in all their company-wide presentations, only to immediately suggest that they were surely going over our silly female heads. Objectively, there is nothing more complicated or of greater consequence about discussing who won the World Series than there is about discussing who put on the most beautiful

wordslut

is a generalization, of course.) But ultimately, it's all a means of talking about "ideas." I took note of a recent conversation among three of my friends, where the topics discussed surfaced in this precise order: social media obsession, sex work, veganism, sobriety, PhD programs, and a current murder trial happening in Downtown Los Angeles. Those sound a lot like "ideas" to me.

The other thing this *people vs. ideas* concept does is contribute to the myth that when women speak to one another, it's "gossip"—which is idle and petty—whereas men's talk is "banter," which is more sophisticated and never stoops to discussing people who aren't in the room. In 2011 language scholar John L. Locke wrote a book called *Duels and Duets: Why Men and Women Talk So Differently*, in which he said, "If [men] have something to say to a foe or competitor, they usually go up to him and say it."

Like Otto Jespersen, Locke had no data to back up this statement. What there is plenty of data to support, however, is the fact that gossip is a serviceable and goal-driven practice. Our linguist Deborah Cameron has explained that when you analyze it closely, gossip serves three main purposes: 1) to circulate personal information in order to keep members of a social group in the know; 2) to bond with one another by establishing the gossipers as an in-group; and 3) to

show at New York Fashion Week; it's simply that the former is generally a more male-centric endeavor and thus perceived as more important. *Blows tiny puff of steam out of ears

affirm the group's commitment to certain values or norms.

This kind of talk is absolutely *not* a women-only pursuit. English-language corpuses offer endless cases of man-on-man gossip. Perhaps the most famous example comes from a conversation most should remember: the recording of Donald Trump and former *Access Hollywood* host Billy Bush talking behind the back of television personality Nancy O'Dell in 2005. I want to point out something important about the linguistic dynamics of this exchange that a lot of political commentators missed. As if I need to remind you, here's the transcript:

DONALD TRUMP: I moved on her like a bitch. But I couldn't get there. And she was married. Then all of a sudden I see her, she's now got the big phony tits and everything. She's totally changed her look.

BILLY BUSH: Sheesh, your girl's hot as shit. In the purple. . . .

TRUMP: Yeah, that's her. With the gold. I better use some Tic Tacs just in case I start kissing her. You know, I'm automatically attracted to beautiful—I just start kissing them. It's like a magnet. Just kiss. I don't even wait. And when you're a star, they let you do it. You can do anything.

BUSH: Whatever you want.

TRUMP: Grab 'em by the pussy.

BUSH: [laughs]

TRUMP: You can do anything.

Back when this tape was released in 2016, everyone from DC to the mainstream media labeled Trump's statements as "lewd commentary" and grotesque "sex boasts"—but those aren't actually the most accurate descriptions of what he's doing. Look closely and you'll see that Trump isn't boasting; he starts by talking about a time he *failed* to seduce a woman. Trump labeled his speech "locker-room banter," which a lot of people took issue with, but it's technically a more spot-on categorization of what he's doing.

"Locker-room banter" is just a manlier-sounding synonym for gossip; it's the act of talking about someone who's not in the room with the intention of establishing camaraderie and in-group norms, just as Deborah Cameron described. This is done by positioning the absent subject of conversation as an outsider and by using embarrassing personal stories and crude language as a currency of trust. Trump starts his exchange not with a boast but with the admission of an unflattering story about a time he wasn't able to convince a woman to have sex with him. He goes on to criticize the woman's appearance (her "big phony tits") and moves on to his "grab 'em by the pussy" line, after which Billy Bush cracks up laughing. Lewd and misogynist as this language is, the main purpose it serves is as a bonding ritual. As Cameron puts it, "Like the sharing of secrets, the sharing of transgressive (or offensive) words like this is a token of intimacy. . . . It says, 'I am showing that I trust you by saying things, and using words, that I wouldn't want the whole world to hear.'" And it's an invitation for the listener to reciprocate. When Trump tells the story about his unsuccessful attempt to have sex with a married woman, the vulnerable confession communicates to Billy Bush that they're buddies who can rely on one another not to tell. Analytically speaking, Trump is gossiping. At some point or another, all men do (though the content is not always this wholly despicable). It's simply that the word *gossip** and its trivial implications have been pegged a feminine thing.

Still, modern linguists agree that woman-to-woman conversation is distinct from man-to-man conversation in a few key ways. In 2004 Jennifer Coates wrote a book called *Women, Men, and Language*, in which she describes a number of tacit techniques observed in all-

---

* The word *gossip* didn't always have such negative (or gendered) connotations: the noun form of gossip originated in Old English with *godsibb*, meaning "god sibling," or the gender-nonspecific godparent of one's child. In part we have Shakespeare to blame for the word's pejoration. He can be found labeling female characters (but never males) *gossips* in a derogatory sense, like in this line from *Titus Andronicus*: "Shall she live to betray this guilt of ours—A long-tongued babbling gossip?"

wordslut

women exchanges that, to contradict Otto Jespersen, actually strike me as linguistically quite "genius" when you look under the surface.

In her book, Coates busts a slew of commonly believed myths about a verbal tactic called *hedging*. When linguists talk about hedges, they're referring to "filler" phrases like *just, you know, well, so, I mean,* and *I feel like*. Tiny as these sound bites are, they're controversial. One of the first modern-language experts to formally censure them was UC Berkeley scholar Robin Lakoff. Back in the 1970s, Lakoff attributed the use of hedges to a sense of hesitancy and lack of confidence. Her idea was that just as society teaches women to express doubt of their physical attractiveness, "a woman has traditionally gained reassurance in this culture from presenting herself . . . as unsure of the correctness of what she's saying." Believing a hesitant style of speech will earn them acceptance, women, says Lakoff, will adopt deferential phrases like *just* and *you know* to dilute the conviction of their statements (e.g., "I <u>just feel like</u> maybe we should push the deadline to Friday, <u>you know</u>?").

Lakoff's issue with women succumbing to this expectation was that inserting too many *justs* or *you knows* in order to come off as sweet and self-doubting won't help women's overall station in society; instead, it will reinforce the stereotype that women are naturally docile and insecure. As a result, they should stop themselves from using these phrases at every turn. If you're a woman, you might have heard a teacher or parent offer similar criticisms at some point in an attempt to help you sound more "authoritative" and "self-confident" for a job interview or presentation.

But linguists have found that there are actually several different types of hedges and don't all serve the same purpose. Men also hedge overall about as frequently as women do, and women hedge to communicate insecurity far less than people assume (all of which we'll get into more in the next chapter). People confuse women's use of certain softening hedges like *just*, *I mean*, and *I feel like* as signs of uncertainty, but research shows that these words accomplish something different: instead, they're used to help create trust and empathy in a conversation. As Coates explains, hedges like these "are used to respect the face needs of all participants, to negotiate sensitive topics, and to encourage the participation of others."

These interpersonal tools are especially handy for women, who almost always dive into sensitive territory at some point during their discussions. Coates collected some enlightening data on how women hedge with one another from a group discussion among female friends about Britain's notorious Yorkshire Ripper case of the early 1980s. The speakers were recalling

wordslut

how, during the hunt for the perpetrator, the police asked the public to consider their family members as suspects. At one point, a woman named Sally revealed that she once thought for a second that the killer might have been her husband. The hedges in her statement are underlined:

"Oh god yes <u>well I mean</u> we were living in Yorkshire at the time and I—<u>I mean</u> I. <u>I mean</u> I did/ I <u>sort of</u> thought <u>well</u> could it be John?"

These hedges here are not representative of Sally's indecision—she isn't hedging or breaking off her sentences due to, as Otto Jespersen said, "talking without having thought out what [she is] going to say." Sally knows exactly what she wants to get across. But because the topic at hand is so sensitive, she needs the *wells* and *I means* so she doesn't come off as brusque and unfeeling. "Self-disclosure of this kind can be extremely face-threatening," Coates explains. "Speakers need to hedge their statements."

This is true in so many situations. For instance, saying something along the lines of, "<u>I mean</u>, I <u>just feel like</u> you should maybe, <u>well</u>, try seeing a therapist" is a gentler, easier-to-hear way of saying, "You should see a therapist." The latter statement, though direct, could come across as cold in the context of a heart-to-heart conversation. The hedged version is more tactful and open, inviting of the listener's point of view, and leaves space for them to interject or share a different perspective (unlike "You should see a therapist," which is closed off and doesn't make room for anyone else's input).

Journalist Ann Friedman has written at length about the hate mail she has received for her perceived overuse of hedges on her podcast *Call Your Girlfriend*, a conversational show she cohosts with her best friend, entrepreneur Aminatou Sow. "Fingernails on a chalkboard" is among the descriptions iTunes reviewers have used to condemn them. In 2015 Friedman defended her language in a piece for *The Cut* that gets to the heart of what linguists know about hedges but that some of Friedman's critics seem to have missed: "Language is not always about making an argument or conveying information in the cleanest, simplest way possible. It's often about building relationships. It's about making yourself understood and trying to understand someone else."

Women's underappreciated prowess in conversation doesn't end with hedges. There are also what linguists call *minimal responses*, which refers to those little phrases like *yeah*, *right*, and *mm-hmm* that one utters while someone else is speaking to demonstrate what Coates terms "active listenership."

In 1995 New Zealand sociolinguist Janet Holmes published a book called *Women, Men and Politeness*, and in it she quoted the following conversation, where two women named Tina and Lyn are talking about a teacher they like. As Tina speaks, watch for Lyn's minimal responses:

wordslut

Well-placed interjections like Lyn's—always at the end of a complete unit of meaning or during a pause—never commandeer the conversation or interrupt its flow. Instead, they work to affirm the speaker while signaling the listener's recognition of how her story is progressing. They're part of what make a conversation feel productive. All the *mm-hmms* and *yeahs* represent Lyn's investment in the discourse and her support of its content. She's an active participant, not simply a wall for Tina to talk at.

These strategic little phrases, Coates says, "illustrate women's sensitive use of minimal responses in talk . . . an achievement which demonstrates the work coparticipants do in predicting how talk will develop." Sonja Lanehart, an African-American language scholar at the University of Texas in San Antonio, told me once that women speakers of African-American Vernacular English (AAVE), a systematic dialect spoken in many black communities, are especially skilled at minimal responses. "If you're sitting in a group of black women, there's going to be a lot of cross talk—a lot of *mm-hmm* and *girl, you're right*," she said. "Black women's speech is so much about consensus and community building."

Another tactic women use to establish conversational connections is a certain form of question-asking that is also misinterpreted as a sign of insecurity. By Lakoff's—and most average English speakers'—measure, when women ask "too many" questions (and these include questions with declarative functions like, "Should we

wordslut

leave for dinner now?" as well as tag questions like "It's a nice day, *isn't it*?"), it always comes from a place of timidity. But Jennifer Coates's research has shown that in women-only spaces, questions (both the declarative and tag kinds) serve the handy, cooperative purposes of introducing new topics, checking the viewpoints of other speakers, and initiating stories. This could manifest itself as, for example, a group of women friends talking about their different experiences with a topic— concerts they've been to, let's say. Everyone could be sharing a story about a time they saw a musician when one speaker targets another in the group and asks her, "Hey, girl, didn't you see Rihanna last year?" or "What was that amazing show you went to with the mosh pit?"

Coates has found that when men ask each other questions (which they do just as frequently as women, though they're never accused of insecurity for it), it's typically to request information and seek answers, but with women, questions serve a different function. Women's intentions are to welcome each participant onto the conversational floor and keep the overall flow moving. The delicate horizontality of all-women discourse requires that no single participant position themselves as the dominant authority on the topic at hand, and the questions they use align with those requirements. "Women's avoidance of information-seeking questions seems to be related to their role in constructing a speaker as 'someone who knows the answer,' an expert," Coates explains. "In friendly conversation, women avoid the role of expert and therefore avoid forms which construct asymmetry."

Women's conversations also have a distinctive turn-taking structure—a style of talk that Coates likens to a musical jam session. "The defining characteristic of a . . . jam session," she says, "is that the conversational floor is potentially open to all participants simultaneously." In such conversations, you might hear overlapping talk, speakers repeating one another, or rephrasing each other's words. Everyone is working together to construct meaning, and thus the one-speaker-at-a-time rule does not apply. "Simultaneous speech does not threaten comprehension," Coates explains, "but on the contrary permits a more multilayered development of topics."

This jam session structure is something you rarely find in exchanges among men. In fact, Coates has found that one of the most defining characteristics of men's conversations, one that helps maintain its hierarchical structure, is that they tend to happen in alternating monologues, or stretches of talk where one speaker holds the floor for a lengthy period of time without any interruptions, not even in the form of minimal responses. This is a way for a speaker to "play the expert," or display their individual knowledge of a subject. "Because most men most of the time choose a one-at-a-time model of turn-taking, overlap is interpreted as deviant, as an (illegitimate) attempt to grab the floor," Coates explains. For this reason, men sometimes interpret women's jam session–style overlaps as rude intrusions. In

wordslut

1992 language scholar Mary Talbot recorded a double date between two heterosexual couples, during which one of the men was telling a story about an airport experience as his partner intermittently chimed in with collaborative comments and support. At a point, the dude finally threw his hands up and said, "I wish you'd stop interrupting me!" If only he'd been a connoisseur of jazz.

Glance at the transcript of almost any all-women conversation and you'll immediately discover what a jam session looks like. For instance, look at the conversation on the following page collected by Jennifer Coates, where she and four other speakers are discussing how apes communicate with language.

This (deliciously nerdy) exchange depicts so many elements of the jam session–esque banter Coates described. Meg, Mary, Bea, and Helen offer minimal responses like *yeah*, *mm-hmm*, and *that's right* to affirm the other speakers and push the discussion forward. We've got Mary and Bea rephrasing one another, finishing each other's sentences, and talking in unison as they discuss how apes refer to a "Brazil nut." Among the many eyeroll-inducing claims he made in *Language*, Otto Jespersen wrote, "the science of language has very few votaries among women." Clearly, he just wasn't paying attention. Luckily, Jennifer Coates was.

As for *why* women tend to talk to one another in this collaborative style: Scholars have posed a few theories. One of the silliest comes from that John L.

MARY: I MEAN THEY CAN SHUFFLE WORDS AROUND AND

MARY: ⌈MAKE A DIFFERENT MEANING/
BEA: ⌊DRAW UP A CONCLUSION

BEA: ((xxx))-
JEN:　　　　THEY PUT TWO WORDS TOGETHER TO FORM A COMPOUND /
MEG:　　　　　　　　　　　　　　YEAH/

MARY:　　　　　　　　　　　　　　　　⌈THAT'S RIGHT=
BEA:　　　　　　　　　　　　　　　　⌊　　　=HMM
JEN: TO MEAN SOMETHING THAT THEY DIDN'T HAVE A LEXICAL TERM FOR

MARY: THAT'S RIGHT　　　　　　　　FOR ⌈ A BRAZIL NUT/
BEA:　　　　　A STONEBERRY FOR A　　⌊ A BRAZIL NUT/
JEN: WHICH IS-
HELEN:　　　RIGHT/

JEN:　　　　　　　　　　　⌈WELL, TH-THEY CAN'T POSSIB⌈LY (HIGH)
MEG: YES AND ⌈LOTIONBERRY FOR ⌊VOMIT/
HELEN: MHM/　⌊GOSH/　　　　　　　　　　　　⌊((WAS IT?))

BEA:　　　　　　　　　　　= LOTIONBERRY FOR WHAT?
JEN: BE IMITATING THEIR TRAINERS=
MEG: YEAH/　　　　　　　　　　　　　　SHE'D- SH-

MEG: SHE'D—SHE'D SICKED UP ONE MORNING ON YOGURT WHICH,

MEG: WOULD HAVE HAD RAISINS IN IT/AND, ER, SHE SAID THAT((IT

MEG: LOOKED)) - THEY ASKED HER WHAT, ER, WHAT THE VOMIT WAS

MEG: AND SHE SAID LOTIONBERRY/
BEA:　　　　　　AH/
HELEN:　　　AMAZING/

wordslut

Locke character, who once suggested that women *naturally* evolved to converse more horizontally, like giraffes evolved to have long necks. His argument is that women's affinities for talking about people behind their backs and babbling over one another in conversation are a product of our ancestors' confinement to domestic spaces—the kitchen, the crafts table—where women were ingrained to develop feelings of closeness through intimate admissions about themselves and other people. So in the kitchens and at the crafts table they shall stay. Locke also argued that men's competitive speech style arose because they were "selected to aggress and dominate, but could end up killing themselves, [so] they needed a safer way of achieving their goals." Thus, men opted for ritualized verbal duels involving words instead of weapons. These confrontations always produced a winner and a loser, and long after dueling traditions ended, men still continue to talk this way. Or so Locke's story goes.

There are less specious explanations for these gendered language differences. One stems from the arguments made by linguist Deborah Tannen in her 1990 best-selling book *You Just Don't Understand: Women and Men in Conversation*. In her book, Tannen claims that from early childhood, women and men are socialized to live in two opposing cultures with two opposing sets of values, so they grow up to understand things differently. Not better or worse, just different. As a result, men's goals when they talk are to communicate information, while women's are to form connections.

Another, more complex theory suggests that women's conversational style has developed as a coping strategy that reflects their position in our culture. This argument is inspired by Janet Holmes, who suggests that our society requires women to be the emotional laborers—shoulders to cry on, carriers of sympathetic burdens. So when women get together and talk to each other in a horizontal style, you're basically looking at a bunch of people all navigating those expectations at the same time, doing a damn good job of it, and enjoying the reciprocation. I think it's safe to say any woman who's ever experienced the genuine empathy and solidarity of another woman knows it's a pretty satisfying feeling.

Now, whether or not women are *born* more empathetic is hard to tell. But experts doubt it. In 2017 gender sociologist Lisa Huebner told *Harper's Bazaar* that we should reject the notion that women are "always, naturally and biologically able to feel, express, and manage our emotions better than men"—and thus should be responsible for doing so. Of course, some people are able to handle emotions better than others because of their individual personalities. But as Huebner says, "I would argue that we still have no firm evidence that this ability is biologically determined."

Some compelling proof that women are indeed *not* born any more capable of empathy or connection than men comes from psychologist Niobe Way. In 2013 Way published a book called *Deep Secrets: Boys' Friendships and the Crisis of Connection*, which explores the friendships of young straight men. Way followed a group of boys from childhood through adolescence and found that when they were little, boys' friendships with other boys were just as intimate and emotional as friendships between girls; it wasn't until the norms of masculinity sank in that the boys ceased to confide in or express vulnerable feelings for one another. By the age of eighteen, society's "no homo" creed had become so entrenched that they felt like the only people they could look to for emotional support were women, further perpetuating the notion that women are obligated by design to carry humanity's emotional cargo.

Natural or not, however, what we know for sure is that wherever women's cooperative speech style comes from, a lot of them seem to be pretty good at it. True, many women don't actively choose to acquire their empathy and collaboration skills, but we can't fault them for making the best of it.

Of course, women don't handle each other with care *all* the time. One amusing illustration of women's linguistic contrariness comes from a 1994 study in which language scholar Gabriella Modan discovered that among Jewish women in particular, the standard "cooperative" model of girl-on-girl conversation doesn't apply. Instead, Jewish women tend to build linguistic solidarity through "opposition" (aka grumpily bickering like siblings). "Oppositional discussion itself creates intimacy because it signals that the relationship is strong enough to withstand serious differences of opinion," Modan wrote.

("Tell me about it," agreed my aunt Francie, one of the Jewish matriarchs of my family, after I summarized this paper for her a few Thanksgivings ago. "I have a couple friends I can barely stand talking to because we disagree on everything. Gotta love 'em.")

There are other ways in which women—Jewish and not—defy linguistic expectations when shielded from the watchful eye of patriarchy. In a 1996 study, Alysa Brown, a language scholar at the University of Texas, San Antonio, taped the natural speech of eight collegiate athletes on a women's tennis team and found that when they were talking just among teammates, there was as much competitive verbal sparring, boasting, and one-upping as you'd typically see in groups of dudes. In one exchange, a woman was telling another teammate how well her last game went, dropping lines like "I was so awesome, I couldn't miss. . . . I just laughed the whole time cause [the other player] sucked so bad." These athletes also used more profanity and fewer cooperative questions. Meanwhile, they spoke in the same interjection-filled jam session manner that Coates found. All things considered, these women displayed a combination of both classically masculine and feminine speech styles.

This idea that women often use both traditionally masculine and feminine conversational tactics is even more intriguing than it sounds, because it raises questions about what feminine speech even is in the first place. Was the source of these athletes' linguistic diversity simply that collegiate sports are a competitive environment that inspires more vulgarity and one-upping? Or was it that out of everywhere in the world, these players felt most comfortable—like they could be their most unfiltered selves—in the company of their teammates, and their speech reflected that? And if that's really the case, what might women's speech sound like if everyone felt that at ease all the time?

Researchers have stumbled upon a few faint glimmers of what women's most unfiltered speech might sound like. Here's one that makes me audibly laugh every time I flip open the transcript: In the 1990s sociologist Jenny Cook-Gumperz recorded a conversation among a trio of three-year-olds in a kindergarten class. The girls were playing "house," casting themselves as the mothers and their dolls as their babies. Acting out domestic scenarios is something that most girls this age do (I know I did)—Cook-Gumperz says that's because the mommy-baby structure allows young girls "to explore their gender roles as women." This makes sense seeing as we live in a culture that has long taught us that being a good mother is part of being a good woman. Playing house is a way to investigate that.

However, because no one is watching too carefully, and because the terribleness that is being a "bad mom" hasn't been fully burned into their brains yet, little girls don't always act like "perfect" mothers in these games. In fact, sometimes they experiment with playing the polar opposite. In Cook-Gumperz's recordings, the three girls are giving their babies baths, when one of them mentions that the water is hot. "Let's boil the babies!" her friend responds. "Yes, let's boil them and boil them!" squeals a third.

This blatantly homicidal and unmotherly exchange between kindergarteners is at once horrifying and hilarious. Eerily, I have a similar memory from my own childhood. One day at preschool, during recess, I remember acting as the mother in one of these domestic games and forcing the girl playing my baby to remain locked in a makeshift dungeon under the slide until I told her she could come out. "I am your master!" I proclaimed. (Did I miss my calling as a dominatrix?)

It's not just kids who talk like this. In 1999 Coates observed a conversation between three British women in their thirties, who'd been close friends for years. In the transcript, they are discussing another friend's poorly behaved kids, specifically how they feel like they're never allowed to say anything negative about them. ("It is undeniable," says Coates, "that one of the burdens of being born female is the imperative to be nice."*) In the privacy of their conversation, however, the women let down their guard, bonding over the unladylike truth that they actually find these children—in their words— "horrible" and "ghastly."

---

* Another fun example of amelioration: Did you know that in Middle English, the word *nice* actually meant foolish or stupid? The word first entered our lexicon via Old French in the twelfth century, when *nice* was meant as a jab for a weak, clumsy simpleton. Over the centuries, it evolved to mean timid, then fussy, then dainty, then careful. It wasn't until the year 1830 when we landed on its current, more positive meaning.

Linguists say these types of mutual confessions serve a larger purpose: to strengthen bonds among women. "Reciprocal admissions of 'not-niceness' . . . [and] taboo feelings . . . reinforce solidarity," Coates explains, labeling these types of exchanges *backstage talk*. "In women's backstage talk, we find women relaxing and letting down the conventional, 'nice' front they normally maintain frontstage. 'Behaving badly' like this backstage—that is, owning our less nice, our more impolite and unsociable feelings—is accepted and even welcomed between friends."

The intention of women's backstage talk is not that different from Donald Trump's lewd banter from the *Access Hollywood* tape—in the end, it is also a means of creating unanimity and closeness. Trump's style of talk is certainly different in other important ways. For one, in locker-room banter, the solidarity doesn't always require a genuine shared confession; sometimes it's simply earned by the crassness of the language itself. For that reason, it might not even matter if the speaker believes what he's saying or not. Trump may have never actually "grabbed" a woman "by the pussy" at all, but in his exchange with Billy Bush, the fact that he would say such a disturbing thing in the first place was the part that counted. I'm willing to bet that at least 50 percent of all the sexist remarks men make in the locker rooms of the world don't reflect actions they've actually taken in real life. In an effort to bond, they descend to their baser selves.

The big problem there is that whether the content of their statements is true or not, the fact that the sexual assault of women is exchanged in casual chitchat (even by otherwise "nice guys") reinforces the idea that that sort of thing is acceptable. As Cameron puts it, "When you objectify and dehumanize a class of people"— whether that's women or a racial minority or both or anyone—"it becomes easier to mistreat them without guilt." Scholars have a clever word for this kind of social structure in which power is formed through a brotherhood that objectifies and dehumanizes those on the outside: they call it *fratriarchy*. Many think this is a more accurate way to describe our culture's post-feudal system, which is ruled not by the fathers, but by peer networks of the brothers. Backstage talk that otherizes all things feminine is part of the mortar that keeps the walls of fratriarchy standing strong. And when you are part of an especially close group, like Donald and his bus bros, it makes it even harder to dissent, because you risk giving up that bond and the power that comes with it. So you end up like Billy Bush, laughing along.

Solidarity among women isn't created this way. Because women are lower on society's totem pole, and have less power to lose, their conversational bonding has everything to do with admitting to their rebellion against the gender status quo, not doing everything they can to live up to it. For that reason, when women build in-group connections through conversation, their statements have to be 100 percent truthful. Otherwise, it wouldn't be a secret worth sharing, and thus, it wouldn't accomplish its goal.

In the end, though, no matter how many studies we do or corpuses we compile, we can never truly know what women's most unmitigated speech sounds like. Even when women feel their most relaxed, society's expectations still loom overhead, and women often check themselves (and one another) for speaking in a way that's too backstage. Coates recalls an example from one of her recordings, where a teenage girl divulges a fantasy about a boy in her class "putting hair gel on his pubic hair and combing it," to which one of her friends exclaims, "Laura!" in a disapproving tone. Pressures for women to position themselves as "normal" and "nice" are almost always a constraint, no matter who's listening. "None of us is ever free of the need to keep up some sort of front," Coates says.

I admit, even if women are able to let down their guards completely in the company of other women, I don't know quite how to feel about the notion that women sometimes reserve certain versions of themselves, of their gender performance, for certain contexts. On the one hand, I think the idea is rather beautiful—that those who've shared a similar experience of the world can get together and use these subtle linguistic cues to connect and feel understood. But at the same time, does that mean we're hiding something outside of those environments?

I'm not the only one with conflicting opinions about

this. Coates is ambivalent too. "It remains to be seen whether the overt expression of alternative and subversive femininities backstage only serves to perpetuate the hetero-patriarchal order, by providing an outlet for the frustrations of frontstage performance," she wrote in 1999. "Or is it possible that such backstage rehearsals may eventually lead to new frontstage performances?"

While writing for a beauty magazine a few years ago, I learned about a makeup artist in her forties who never went to bed without a full face of makeup on. Her husband never saw her without lipstick, eyeshadow, mascara, the works. She didn't want him to see her as anything less than her most polished self. She exhaustively put forth a frontstage performance from the neck up, even at four in the morning.

If letting yourself boast about your victories, tell off-color stories, and express disapproval of children are the equivalents of showing your un-made-up face, I'm curious to know what would happen if women all agreed to retire their mascara wands, if for no other reason than to let the overconfident Otto Jespersens and John L. Lockes of the world know that we're capable of being just as great and just as crude as men. If not greater and cruder.

Male linguists certainly aren't the only ones cocksure of their beliefs about women's speech. False and disparaging conclusions are drawn about how women use language, especially young women, by all different kinds of people every day. Have you ever had someone tell you that you should stop using the word *like* because it makes you sound stupid? Or that you shouldn't apologize so much? If you're a woman under the age of thirty-five, odds are you have. Perhaps you've even passed one of these judgments yourself. I wouldn't blame you if you did—we English speakers have been trained to turn our noses up at any type of speech that doesn't sound like that of a male thirty-four-year-old TV host named Billy, or, as we'll learn in a second, a sixty-four-year-old NPR reporter named Bob.

Today's sharpest linguists, however, have data suggesting that "teenage girl speak," one of the most loathed and mocked language styles, is actually what standard English is going to sound like in the near future. In a lot of ways, it's already happening. And that's making a lot of middle-age men very, very cranky.

women didn't ruin the english language— they, like, invented it

It's 2013, and Bob Garfield is in a state of exaspera-
tion. "Vulgar," he spits into his microphone. "Repulsive."
I'm listening to an episode of the NPR host's language-
themed podcast, *Lexicon Valley*. Though I cannot see
fifty-eight-year-old Garfield with my own eyes, from
the disdain in his voice, I can picture him, scornfully
stroking his frosty-white facial hair and crossing one
corduroy-clad arm over the other. The topic of discussion is a linguistic phenomenon that Garfield says is so
endlessly "annoying" that he wishes he could "wave a
magic wand over a significant portion of the American
public and make it come to an end." It is an oddity that

wordslut

occurs "exclusively" among young women, he tells co-host Mike Vuolo with conviction. "I don't have any data [proving this]," he says. "I simply know I'm right."*

Any guesses as to what this odious feminine speech quality could be? It's *vocal fry*, also known by linguists as *creaky voice*. You may have heard of this phenomenon or even do it yourself: vocal fry is a raspy, low-pitched noise that we often hear as people trail off at the ends of their sentences. The sound is produced when a speaker compresses their vocal cords, reducing the airflow and frequency of vibrations through the larynx, causing the voice to sound sort of, well, creaky. Like a rusty door, or the grate of a Mexican guiro. (Commentators like to reference the voices of Valley girls and Kim Kardashian when describing vocal fry—in fact, it is a part of a legitimate dialect colloquially termed "Valley girl speak"—though people of all genders and geographical locations do it too, which I'll get into later.)

Garfield says that in recent years, he's noticed a vocal fry epidemic in the speech of women in their teens and twenties—nothing but a "mindless affectation"—and he is certain that it's irreparably ruining the English language. To demonstrate the sound, Garfield beckons his eleven-year-old daughter to the microphone. "Ida, be obnoxious," he instructs.

In the years following this podcast, vocal fry becomes

---

* Columbia University linguist John McWhorter took over *Lexicon Valley* in 2016, and thankfully he cares very much about collecting data before claiming to be right about something.

increasingly mauled and mocked by the media—a public emblem of young women's overall inability to communicate as elegantly as older, wiser men. In 2014 the *Atlantic* publishes a report that women who talk with vocal fry are less likely to be hired. In 2015 a male *Vice* reporter publishes a story called "My Girlfriend Went to a Speech Therapist to Cure Her Vocal Fry." The same year, journalist Naomi Wolf pens an article for the *Guardian* titled, "Young women, give up the vocal fry and reclaim your strong female voice." She writes, "'Vocal fry' is that guttural growl at the back of the throat, as a Valley girl might sound if she had been shouting herself hoarse at a rave all night."

I myself remember being berated for using vocal fry in high school by a male theater teacher who told me that

VOCAL FRY IS THE FUTURE, SORRYYYYYYY

VOCAL CORDS

women didn't ruin the english language—they, like, invented it

if I continued contaminating my lines with creak, I would never make it to Broadway. (Could this be the reason I was not cast as one of the original stars of *Hamilton*?)

Of course vocal fry isn't the only thing wrong with young female voices. Around the same time of Bob Garfield's episode, the internet has a collective freak-out over contemporary "lady language," and journalists everywhere start cranking out think pieces analyzing other characteristics commonly noticed and reviled in women's speech. Saying *like* after every other word is a well-known example. So is apologizing too much; using hyperbolic internet slang ("OMG, I AM LITERALLY DYING"); and speaking with uptalk, where you end a declarative sentence with the upward intonation of a question.

Suddenly, making poorly informed, pseudofeminist claims about how women talk becomes the trendy thing for brands and magazines to do. In 2014 hair care company Pantene releases an advertisement encouraging women to stop saying "sorry" all the time. (Because now not only does your hair need a makeover, so does your speech!) A year later, publications like *Time* and *Business Insider* begin claiming that uptalk makes women sound timid and self-conscious. *YOUNG LADY, IF YOU EVER WANT A JOB OR A HUSBAND YOU MUST STOP TALKING THIS WAY*, the internet screams.

At the height of this media frenzy, I was a twenty-something female, the very target of these articles and commercials, and I had three concerns: 1) whether or not speech qualities like vocal fry and uptalk are *really* exclusive to young women; 2) the purpose they serve, if so; and 3) why everybody hates them so much.

Those hair product copywriters and magazine reporters thought they were original, but when it comes to telling young women how they should and shouldn't speak, UC Berkeley's Robin Lakoff had them beat by about four decades. Lakoff's most famous contribution in that 1975 book of hers, *Language and Woman's Place*, was a list of observed characteristics of "women's speech." This was basically Otto Jespersen's "The Woman" chapter with a quasi-feminist twist. Lakoff's inventory of lady language included: a tendency to over-apologize, "empty" adjectives ("This chocolate mousse is *heavenly*"), ultrapolite language ("Would you mind if . . ."), strong emphasis ("I *LOVE* that show"), indirect requests ("I think the package is still downstairs," instead of, "Can you go get the package?"), hypercorrection of grammar ("between you and I," as opposed to "between you and me"), hedging ("kind of," "you know"), tag questions ("That movie was good, *wasn't it*?"), and an avoidance of cursing ("Goodness gracious" instead of "Holy shit").

Lakoff's argument was that women systematically use these linguistic features more than men because they have been socialized to do so as a part of the cultural expectation that women present themselves as deferential and unassertive. What was good about Lakoff's commentary was that it brought an unprecedented amount of attention to the relationship between

women didn't ruin the english language—they, like, invented it

wordslut

language and social power, and she was on the right track in helping to illuminate ways in which speech can perpetuate existing gender stereotypes. Never before had a linguist formally argued that the types of intonation or questions one uses could send messages about the speaker's gender, thus granting or impeding their access to respect and authority. Where Lakoff went wrong, however, was suggesting that women acclimate to men's speech style if they want any hope of equality. According to Lakoff, weakness is a trait we've come to strongly (albeit unfairly) associate with being female, not just verbally but in general; so, if women would like to be perceived otherwise, it would behoove them to dissociate themselves from what we've been conditioned to see as feminine behavior. That means making an effort to avoid speaking with any of the characteristics listed earlier, which Lakoff claimed made women sound insecure, just like all those commercials and articles forty years later.

Fortunately, sociolinguistics has come a long way since Lakoff's book, and there are plenty of twenty-first-century language experts who've taken "Valley girl" speak seriously enough to figure out what it actually is. One of these scholars is Carmen Fought, a linguist from Pitzer College (who, incidentally, has one of the butteriest, most soothing speaking voices I've ever heard). As Fought says, "If women do something like uptalk or vocal fry, it's immediately interpreted as insecure, emotional, or even stupid." But the truth is much more interesting: Young women use the linguistic features that they do, not as mindless affectations, but as power tools for establishing and strengthening relationships. Vocal fry, uptalk, and even *like*, are in fact not signs of ditziness, but instead all have a unique history and specific social utility. And women are not the only people who use them.

In many languages around the world, vocal fry is not some random quirk—it is built into their very phonology. For instance, in Kwak'wala, a Native American language, the word for *day* cannot be pronounced *without* using creak, or else it wouldn't make sense (kind of like pronouncing the English word *day* without the *y*). What's interesting about English speakers' use of vocal fry is that early studies actually attributed the speech quality primarily to men. One of the first official observations of vocal fry in English was made by a UK linguist in the 1960s, who determined that it was British *dudes* who employed vocal fry as a way of communicating a higher social standing. There was also an American study of creaky voice in the 1980s that called the phenomenon "hyper-masculine" and a "robust marker of male speech." Many linguists also agree that using a bit of creak at the ends of sentences has been happening in the United States among English speakers of all genders, with no fuss or fallout, for decades.

But in the mid-2000s, folks started noticing an increase of vocal fry usage in the voices of American college-age women, but not so much in their male

08

calassmates. Researchers were intrigued, so they decided to take a gander and see if these observations were accurate. Long story short, they were: in 2010, linguistics scholar Ikuko Patricia Yuasa published a study showing that American women use vocal fry about 7 percent more than American men. And we've been getting creakier ever since.

But, like, why? What is vocal fry good for? (Other than to annoy beardy old guys, that is.) As it turns out, a bunch of things. First, Yuasa points out that since vocal fry is so very low in pitch, it could be a way for women to compete with men's voices—to sound more authoritative. "Creaky voice may provide a growing number of American women with a way to project an image of accomplishment, while retaining female desirability," she wrote in her study. Personally, I have found myself unconsciously dropping into vocal fry during presentations at work to convey this sort of laid-back authority. "You always sound like you know what you're talking about to me," said my boss when I asked her if I ever came off as insecure during meetings. (Then again, she's a woman in her twenties too.)

On the flip side, Mark Liberman, a linguist at the University of Pennsylvania, told the *New York Times* in 2012 that vocal fry can also be used to convey a sense of disinterest in a topic (which, as a teenage girl, I certainly loved to do). "It's a mode of vibration that happens when the vocal cords are relatively lax. . . . So maybe some people use it when they're relaxed and even bored," he said. Like a subtle way of telling someone you find them unstimulating.

To sum things up, over the first two decades of the twenty-first century, women began speaking with increasingly lower-pitched voices, attempting to convey more dominance and expressing more boredom—all things that middle-aged men have historically not been in favor of women doing. Perhaps this could explain why Bob Garfield and his peers have scrutinized vocal fry so mercilessly?

Like and uptalk are two more subjects of deep linguistic ridicule—they are probably also the most recognizable aspects of Valley girl speak. When making fun of teenage girls, imitators go for these sorts of phrases: "I, like, went to the movies? And I was like, *'I want to see Superwoman?'* But Brad was like, *'No way?'* So we, like, left." (I'm not certain why people love satirizing teen girls so much, but my theory is that it's just an excuse to speak in this highly entertaining fashion.)

Despite the word's detractors, *like* is in fact extremely useful and versatile. Alexandra D'Arcy, Canadian linguist at the University of Victoria, has dedicated much of her research to identifying and understanding the many functions of *like*. D'Arcy ebulliently describes her work for UVic's YouTube channel: "*Like* is a little word that we really, really don't like at all—and we want to blame young girls, who we think are destroying the language," she explains. But the truth is that *like* has been a part of English for more than two hundred years. "We can find speakers today in their seventies, eighties, and nineties around little villages in the United Kingdom, for example," D'Arcy says with a smile, "who use *like* in many of the same ways that young girls today are using it."

According to D'Arcy, there are six completely distinct forms of the word *like*. The two oldest types in English are the adjective *like* and the verb *like*. In the sentence, "I like your suit, it makes you look like James Bond," the first *like* is a verb and the second is an adjective—and even the crabbiest English speakers are fine with both. Today, these two *likes* sound exactly the same, so most people don't even notice that they're different words with separate histories. They're homonyms, just how the noun *watch* (meaning the timepiece on your wrist) and the verb *watch* (meaning what you do with your eyes when you turn on the TV) are homonyms. The *Oxford English Dictionary* says that the verb *like* comes from the Old English term *lician*, and the adjective comes from the Old English *lich*. The two converged at some point over the last eight hundred or so years, giving us lots of time to get used to them.

But four new *likes* developed much more recently than that—and D'Arcy says these are all separate words with distinct uses, as well. Only two of these *likes* are used more frequently by women, and only one of them is thought to have been masterminded by young Southern California females in the 1990s. That one would be the quotative *like*, which you hear in, "I was like, '*I want to see Superwoman.*'" As lampooned as it is, pragmatically speaking, this *like* is one of my favorites because it allows you to tell a story, to relay something that happened, without having to quote the interaction verbatim. For example, in the sentence "My boss was like, 'I need those papers by Monday,' and I was like, 'Are you fucking kidding me?'" you're not repeating what you truly said but instead using *like* to convey what you wanted to say or how you felt in the interaction. Thanks, Valley girls. This very useful quotative *like* continues to explode in common usage.

The other *like* that women tend to use more frequently is categorized as a *discourse marker* and can be found in contexts such as, "Like, this suit isn't even new." A discourse marker—sometimes called a filler word—is a type of phrase that can help a person connect, organize, or express a certain attitude with their speech. Other discourse markers include the hedges we learned about in the last chapter, like *just*, *you know*, and *actually*.

There are two last forms of *like*: one is an adverb, which is used to approximate something, as in the sentence, "I bought this suit like five years ago." As of the 1970s this *like* has largely replaced the approximate adverb *about* in casual conversation, and it has always been used equally among men and women (so it isn't hated as much). And last, there's the *discourse particle like*, which we hear in, "I think this suit is like my favorite possession." This like is similar to the discourse marker, except that it's not used in quite the same way syntactically or semantically; plus, dudes use it just as much as women do (D'Arcy doesn't know quite why that is), though they're almost never ridiculed for it.

Objectively, we can see that using one, two, or all of these different *likes* in the same sentence isn't inherently bad. As a matter of fact, some studies have demonstrated that speech lacking in *likes* and *you knows* can sound too careful, robotic, or unfriendly. So next time someone accuses you of saying *like* too much, feel free to ask them, "Oh really? Which kind?" Because D'Arcy says that ordinary speakers tend to buy into the Valley girl stereotype so hardcore, blaming young women for all of these *likes*, simply because they don't notice the differences among them.

Uptalk is the other disfavored feature of teen girl speak that, as it turns out, is quite practical when you look closely. Linguists say uptalk made its splash into everyday conversation in the 1980s and '90s—the era of *Fast Times at Ridgemont High* and *Clueless*. This time line contributes to the much-believed lore that uptalk is another Valley girl invention (so much credit given to such a small group of people!). In reality, it's believed to have been stolen from Australia. That high-rising terminal is a classic characteristic of Aussie dialects—we forget that "G'day, mate?" is not actually a question.

Over the past twenty years, everyone from corporate executives to high school English teachers have criticized uptalk for sounding unassertive. I even had a linguist admit to me that she's not a fan—"It's unfortunately true that even I don't like uptalk," NYU professor Louise O. Vasvári whispered to me over the phone, a twinge of guilt in her voice. "I think it makes women sound insecure because it sounds like they're asking questions. I'm not supposed to say this."

But no matter how people feel personally about uptalk, studies have shown that in certain contexts, it's actually used to convey the *opposite* of insecurity.

Consider a University of Pennsylvania study from 1991, which looked at a Texan sorority and found that senior members often used uptalk to assert power over juniors. ("There's a very important Greek event tomorrow? And we expect everyone to attend?") Lakoff once theorized that one reason why women might use a question-esque intonation when communicating authority is because they've trained themselves to, either on purpose or subconsciously, so they don't come off as "bossy" or "bitchy." By Lakoff's account, uptalk allows women to express confidence without being attacked for not sounding "ladylike." In my own speech, I have noticed that I'll use uptalk to soften a declarative sentence, especially when discussing a topic that's a bit controversial, but I don't think it's necessarily to seem less bitchy. Instead, it feels like a way for me to state an opinion confidently while at the same time opening myself up for others' responses. Which I don't think is necessarily a bad thing?

Uptalk is by no means exclusive to women's speech. A 2005 study conducted in Hong Kong, which examined

wordslut

the intonation patterns of English-speaking business professionals and academics in meetings, found that the meeting chairs (aka the highest-ranking people in the room) used uptalk as much as seven times more than their subordinates. Here, uptalk was also used to assert dominance—to pressure listeners to pay attention, get on the same page, and respond. But this time, nobody misinterpreted it as insecurity, because most of the speakers were men.

These misconceptions that women use uptalk more than men do and that it's always used to express insecurity are very similar to the myths commonly believed about how women use hedges, like *just*, *you know*, and *like*. A series of studies on hedges from the late twentieth century revealed that overall, the statistical significance between men's and women's total frequency of hedging is almost nonexistent. Plus, not all hedges serve the same purpose. Take the case of *you know*: linguists have discovered that not only do men and women use this phrase in equal numbers, but that in many instances, women actually use it as a way to communicate active *confidence*. In the 1980s our New Zealand linguist Janet Holmes analyzed a large corpus of speech and found that when used with a rising, question-like intonation, *you know* does indeed connote hesitancy or doubt ("It's not, you know, fair."), but, when spoken with a flat intonation ("It's not fair, you know."), it does just the reverse. Holmes's numbers demonstrated that the total number of *you knows* collected were almost identical between genders, but women used the phrase with a flat pitch, communicating confidence, over 20 percent more than men. And yet, most people don't hear it that way*—at the first sign of a woman hedging, they automatically assume insecurity.

The only type of hedge young women really do use more frequently than men is the discourse marker *like*, but again, it's not due to insecurity. Studies on adolescent speech indicate that young people hedge with *like* in order to "partially detach themselves from the force of utterances that could be considered evaluative, either positively evaluative of self or negatively evaluative of others." Our genderlect expert Jennifer Coates postulates that men might use this type of *like* less overall due to their choices of conversational subject. "Unlike female speakers, male speakers on the whole avoid sensitive topics," she says. By and large, men do not self-disclose or

---

* The same sentiment is true of tag questions: in the 1980s, Deborah Cameron conducted a pair of studies at Oxford proving that tag questions are highly nuanced and can serve over half a dozen different purposes depending on the interaction and dynamic between participants. Gender has almost nothing to do with *how many* tags one uses, and while gender has something to do with the *type* of tags used, a person's level of power in an interaction is way more relevant. Better yet, the specific types of tags women favored were actually associated with *more* power, not less. The study showed that women use more "facilitative" tags, which express interest and solidarity, and invite other speakers into the conversation (e.g., "*Game of Thrones* was great last night, wasn't it?"). Facilitative tags are also consistently used by people in so-called powerful interactional positions, regardless of gender, like courtroom judges and talk show hosts. Meanwhile, men are shown to use more "modal" tags, which humbly request information ("John Quincy Adams was the fourth US president, right?"). Equally, there is a pattern associating modal tags with "powerless" speakers (like classroom students and defendants on the witness stand). This is also regardless of gender.

talk about personal matters as liberally. Thus, the need for this particular hedge does not apply.

So why is it that young women get the harshest dose of criticism for vocal fry, uptalk, *like*, and other hedges? According to linguists, the way that these speech qualities are perceived has way less to do with the thing being said and way *more* to do with who's saying it. In other words, judgments about linguistic prestige depend a whole lot on how we feel about the speaker. A study from 2010 conducted by two linguists from Stanford University and UC Santa Cruz found that participants who listened to someone positioned as a political "expert" did not interpret the person's uptalk as a sign of insecurity. But when the uptalker was introduced as a "nonexpert," listeners questioned their competence. UPenn linguist Mark Liberman says that even one of our American presidents was known to uptalk. "George W. Bush used to do it," he recalls. "And nobody ever said, 'Oh, that GWB is so insecure, just like a young girl.'" (Although, to be fair, that was the least of W's problems.)

Over the past two decades, vocal fry, uptalk, and *like* have transcended genders and generations. Brian Reed, thirtysomething host of the blockbuster 2017 podcast *S-Town*, used uptalk just as much as any female podcaster I've ever listened to. There have also been formal studies of *Jeopardy!* contestants and dads at Jamba Juice that show that modern dudes definitely uptalk like crazy. I've heard my sixty-one-year-old father, a neuroscientist, use vocal fry hundreds of times. And according to a 2003 analysis Liberman did of phone conversation recordings, men overall use *like* in its many forms more frequently than women do.

People don't seem to care or even notice when men talk this way. Only when it comes from female mouths does it cause such an upset. This fact makes it clear that our culture's aversion to vocal fry, uptalk, and *like* isn't really about the speech qualities themselves. Instead, it's about the fact that, in modern usage, women were the first to use them.

For decades, linguists have agreed that young, urban females tend to be our linguistic innovators. As South Korea is to beauty products and Silicon Valley is to apps, women in their teens, twenties, and thirties create—and/ or incubate—future language trends. (Though not on purpose or for money.) "It's generally pretty well known that if you identify a sound change in progress, then young people will be leading old people, and women tend to be maybe half a generation ahead of males," Liberman says. (Fun fact: linguists have also determined that the *least* innovative language users are nonmobile, older, rural males, which they've majestically given the acronym "NORMs.")

Exactly *why* women seem to move language forward like this is not as clear. One hypothesis is that women are simply given more freedom in society to talk with pizzazz. Studies of internet slang have shown women to use language more expressively: creative punctuation, descriptive hashtags, emoji, and fun abbreviations like OMG and AF. Another theory is that women are more attuned to social interactions and thus likelier to pick up on subtle linguistic cues. But to me, the most compelling argument is that young women innovate because they see language as a tool to assert their power in a culture that doesn't give them a lot of ways to do that.

Language can be an empowering resource for women who wish to move up in the world; it has been for generations. A striking example: In 1978 award-winning linguist Susan Gal traveled to Austria to study a small, poor Hungarian-speaking village that had ended up on Austrian soil due to how the borders changed after World War I. This border shift was bad luck for these Hungarian villagers, because now they were forced to live in a country where everyone else spoke German. So, the women—the young women at least—began learning it. This was a smart move because having some German under their belts would allow them to leave the village, get better jobs, marry hot Austrian husbands if they were into that sort of thing, and generally climb the socioeconomic stepladder. Gal noticed that it was too late for the old women to make this move, but for those who had the chance, language was a way to escape the community and have a better life.

This story jives with Louise O. Vasvári's theory that young women in poorer communities, as well as young immigrant women, are more likely to need language for social mobility. Why? Generally, dudes have better access to blue-collar jobs, which have traditionally paid more than many working-class jobs for women. "Historically, in coal-mining areas, a miner would make more money in a week than his waitress girlfriend would make in a month," Vasvári explains. A woman *could* theoretically get a coal mining job, and many have, but the work is brutal and the social environment unwelcoming. So, for a woman to earn more dough in a culturally acceptable manner, she would have to get what is called a "pink-collar" job, like a receptionist or bank teller. And these sorts of jobs require new language skills, whether that means learning a more "prestigious" dialect or an entirely new language. As Vasvári recalls, "There was a study in Spain where women were learning Catalan because they wanted to be able to go out and get a secretary job, and the men would actually make fun of them for becoming bilingual."

People have looked down upon the way women use language for centuries, and like Otto Jespersen and Bob Garfield, they often write off women's communication styles as stupid and annoying. But observers of gender and foreign language have noticed that when there truly is a significant difference between how men and women talk, it's often because women were literally forbidden from using certain words, sounds, or writing systems and were thus forced to innovate. For instance, in some of southern Africa's Bantu languages, there is a strict rule that forbids married women from saying the name of their father-in-law, or any word that sounds similar or has the same root. Bantu women often work their way around this rule by borrowing synonyms from other local languages. Some linguists think that is actually how click consonants made their way into Bantu—women borrowed them from the Khoisan languages of West Africa, and eventually they made their way into the mainstream Bantu spoken by everyone. A similar story comes from China, where the Chinese writing style Nüshu is often referred to as a "women's language" and regarded as completely separate from standard Chinese script. In reality, though, Nüshu is simply a different, more phonetic way of writing standard Chinese, which women developed at a time when they weren't allowed to learn to read and write.

Both of these examples are what Deborah Cameron calls "a tribute to women's ingenuity but also a product of their historically subordinate status." For women, language is often a complex way of coping with, or all-out resisting, oppression.

In situations like Nüshu, the German-speaking Hungarians, and the Catalan-speaking Spaniards, it's clear why young women innovate linguistically—it's their ticket out. As for why they are responsible for things like vocal fry? A foolproof conclusion has yet to be drawn. However, Vasvári muses that this might be linked to the idea that language can also serve as a form of symbolic agency. Women aren't the only people who use language this way. "Compare how so much of slang and other new usages had their origin in black English,"

Vasvári offers, referencing popular terms like *phat* and *fuckboy*, which have been swiped, however unwittingly, from AAVE. "You can wonder why it is that the language of a powerless group gets taken up later by the majority—but perhaps it has always been the powerless who use language as a form of power. Think of disenfranchised Jews in Europe, who gave origin to 'the Jewish joke' and, in fact, to much of humor altogether."

The ways in which women and many other socially oppressed folks empower themselves with language are all rather connected. There exists a long history of marginalized groups innovating linguistically to build themselves up. And they're clearly very good at it, because the rest of the world invariably ends up talking just like them, whether they know whom to credit for all their cool new slang terms, word pronunciations, and intonations or not.

There is another reason why society loves crapping on uptalk, *like*, and other feminine speech qualities, even though it winds up adopting them: simply put, people get freaked out when things change beyond their control. See, when NORMs like Bob Garfield start hearing vocal fry at the ends of young women's sentences, they have a mini existential crisis. "[They] become critical and maybe even disturbed and say, 'That's not how the language is supposed to sound!'" says Auburn Barron-Lutzross, a linguist at UC Berkeley. Because these guys are used to being in charge, when someone else starts making things happen, they feel like the end of the world

women didn't ruin the english language—they, like, invented it

wordslut

is nigh. "Had NORMs been the ones to pioneer vocal fry, uptalk, and *like*, we'd be praising them as enriching expansions of the language. We'd be reading *The, Like, New Yorker*," journalist Gabriel Arana told the *Atlantic*. But they didn't—and since America tends to listen to old white dudes, it takes a little while for all of us to catch on.

There is a simple way we can be part of the shift toward a less judgmental linguistic future: instead of acting crotchety and pedantic toward new language trends, we can feel curious and fascinated by them. Whenever we get the urge to criticize women or anyone else (even our own selves) for a certain dialect feature, we can remember to think like a linguist, reminding ourselves that systematic speech patterns are almost never mindless or stupid. Believing that they are only reinforces a screwed-up linguistic standard.

Think about the act of policing women's voices—their intonation, their syntax, their word choice—in the same way we think about policing women's appearance. Just how women's magazine articles and commercials tell them they need to be prettier, they also tell them they need to talk differently. I've heard the satirical argument that women were given purses to hold and high heels to wear to physically slow them down. While I don't take this sentiment literally, I think you can compare it to the critique of women's voices, which are there to steal the focus away from the content of their statements, while distracting women with the anxiety of how their speech sounds to other people. Fretting over the amount of creak in your voice or number of times you apologize are the linguistic equivalents of worrying if your forehead is shiny or if you're spilling out of your Spanx.

And gently advising women to stop using discourse markers and vocal fry so they can sound more "articulate"—no matter how well intentioned—is not helpful either. In 2016 I was offered a promo code to test out a new voice-recognition app designed to help young people practice talking without filler phrases like *you know* and *like*, so they could sound more "authoritative." But dressing up this advice as empowering is as shady as telling a woman that wearing a longer hemline will make her worthier of success. It's a way of punishing women for their own oppression. One of our culture's least helpful pieces of advice is that women need to change the way they speak to sound less "like women" (or that queer people need to sound straighter, or that people of color need to sound whiter). The way any of these folks talk isn't inherently more or less worthy of respect. It only sounds that way because it reflects an underlying assumption about who holds more power in our culture.

As Deborah Cameron once said, "Teaching young women to accommodate to the linguistic preferences, aka prejudices, of the men who run law firms and engineering companies is doing the patriarchy's work for it." It accepts the idea that "feminine" speech is the problem, rather than the sexist attitudes toward it. "The

business of feminism is surely to challenge sexist attitudes," Cameron continues, "to work against prejudice,
not around it."

So, if someone ever tries to make you—or anyone
else—feel stupid for pushing your vocal folds together
at the ends of sentences, saying *sorry* a lot, or another
language feature they've decided they don't like, remember: even if the NORMs don't get you, linguists will.
After all, deep down, the haters are probably just bitter
that you're changing the world in ways they can't control or understand.

I know that sounds kind of dramatic. But, like, it's
important?

5

how to embarrass the shit out of people who try to correct your grammar

Everyone I've ever known has at least one grammar pet peeve. A 2013 BuzzFeed listicle titled "17 Misused and Made-Up Words That Make You Rage" features common blunders such as "irregardless," "supposably," and the phrase "I could care less," each paired with a gif of someone tearing their hair out or screaming into the sky. My twenty-five-year-old brother recently told me that one of his greatest pet peeves is when people respond to the question of "How are you?" with "I'm well," instead of "I'm good."

"It just sounds so stupid." He chuckled.

I'm not proud to say that I too reflexively cringe

whenever I hear this common grammar infraction. But I try not to blame the speaker. "I'm well" is an example of something called hypercorrection, which refers to the over-application of some perceived grammar rule that results in a sentence that sounds right but technically isn't. Saying "you and I" where "me and you" should go (as in, "Let's keep this between you and I") is another example, as is dropping an erroneous "whom" in place of "who," like in the sentence, "Whomever drank my Diet Coke needs to replace it by tomorrow, or else."*

Everyone loves that "gotcha" feeling that comes with catching someone in a grammar violation, especially when you know the speaker was trying to sound smart to begin with. The thing about hypercorrection, though, is that the intentions are usually noble. Linguists have found that hypercorrection is most common among lower-middle-class women, who see the adverb *well*, for instance, as a marker of higher social class (you'd be more likely to hear a Goldman Sachs exec say "He knows the market well," not "He knows the market good"). As we learned from the last chapter, acquiring more prestigious language skills is a powerful tool for women of less socioeconomic privilege. To manifest their aspirations of upward mobility, they attempt to adopt the higher-class grammatical form, but they overshoot the target. The misused *wells* and *whoms* were intended to

---

* Taken from an actual note I saw once on the fridge at a former job. (I didn't steal the soda, I swear.)

hoist the speaker up the socioeconomic ladder—to gain her respect. It just doesn't always work out that way.

"Well, now I feel bad, when you put it like that," my brother said after I explained all this.

"Just something to think about," I told him.

My brother's instinct to judge people by their adverb misusage is hardly uncommon. In fact, condemning others' grammar is one of the most universally accepted snobberies in Western culture. "When the subject is language, you can take pride in being a snob," Deborah Cameron once said. "You can even display your exquisite sensitivity by comparing yourself to a genocidal fascist ('I'm a bit of a grammar Nazi: I can't bear it when people use language incorrectly')."

There is at least one type of person you are guaranteed never to find correcting a person's grammar, however: a linguist. That sounds counterintuitive, but language scientists aren't interested in how language *should* work; they're interested in how it *does* work. (Policing one's grammar in public is what Deborah Cameron calls "a shitty thing to do.") People tend to think of prescriptive grammar—that's the grammar your English teacher made you learn—as this almighty, unchanging force that has been there forever, like gravity or the sun. We forget that grammar rules are a human invention, and they're constantly evolving. What's considered "good grammar" today might have been totally unacceptable fifty years ago, or vice versa.

wordslut

Recall the word *ain't*, which was once associated with high-class Brits—Winston Churchill was a fan—and has simply devolved since the early twentieth century to become one of the most stigmatized grammatical forms in English history.

Sociologically speaking, there are certain grammatical rules across the world's many languages that carry a load of baggage way heavier than any grammar guide. Some of the most common grammar constructions that speakers use every day and take for granted—nouns, adjectives, suffixes, etc.—are secretly informing their conscious thoughts about human gender. So the next time your coworker, your sibling, or some jerk on Twitter tries to ridicule your adverb usage, you're going to want to have this information at the ready.

In about a quarter of the world's languages, gender and gender stereotypes are fundamentally built into the grammar system. You're probably familiar with a language in which every noun gets a gender assignment—English isn't one of them, but French, Spanish, and tons of others are. In these languages, every noun belongs to a masculine or feminine "noun class," which might affect the prefix or suffix of the word. (There are also languages that have a "neuter" noun class, and some languages have as many as twenty other categories, based on qualities like animate vs. inanimate, edible vs. nonedible, and rational vs. irrational, which we'll get into shortly.) A noun's gender assignment extends to other modifiers in the sentence, like adjectives and past-tense verbs, whose genders have to "agree" with the noun.

In the French sentence *Le diner est sur la table verte*, which means "dinner is on the green table," the word for *dinner* is masculine, but *table* is feminine, as is *green*, the adjective describing the table. In the Spanish sentence *El nuevo jefe necesita una recepcionista*, meaning, "The new boss needs a receptionist," the noun *boss* is masculine, as is the adjective *new*, which describes the boss, while the word for *receptionist* is feminine. (And if the gender assignments in that Spanish example seem sketchy to you, you're onto something.)

This system of noun classification is called "grammatical gender."

We don't assign gender to nouns in English—except, that is, when we use the pronoun *she* to refer to natural disasters, countries, and cars (all of which, by no coincidence, are dangerous things that men feel the need to vanquish and control; more on that in a bit). We do, however, have a system called "natural gender," which means that the only gendered nouns in our language (*man, woman, brother, sister, king, queen, actor, actress,* etc.) ostensibly correspond to the sex of the person we're talking about, as do our singular third-person pronouns: *he* and *she*.*

---

* Cornell linguist Sally McConnell-Ginet has pointed out that in English, "natural gender" is really a misnomer, since in many cases, the gendered words we use to describe someone (or something) do not

wordslut

People like to think grammatical gender and "natural" gender have nothing to do with each other—just because a noun is classified as masculine in Spanish or French doesn't mean the literal thing is masculine. In many cases, this is true. Certainly no one thinks that because the Spanish word for *eye* (*ojo*) is masculine and the word for *chin* (*barbilla*) is feminine, Spanish speakers perceive eyes as inherently macho body parts and chins as inherently ladylike ones.

But toward the end of the twentieth century, linguist Suzanne Romaine determined that this relationship between grammatical and "natural" gender is not always so separate. In 1997 Romaine published a seminal* paper called *"Gender, Grammar, and the Space in Between."* The same year of Princess Diana's death and Mike Tyson's bite fight, Romaine was blowing minds at the University of Oxford with the theory that in languages all over the world, there is some undeniable "leakage" going on between grammatical gender and how we perceive human gender in real life. Romaine's main point is that in languages with masculine and feminine noun classifications (from Spanish to Sanskrit), it is highly

describe a noun's "natural sex" but instead our interpretation of its gender. For this reason, she suggests we rename our system "notional gender." I'm on board with this concept, but for our purposes, I'm going to stick to using the term "natural gender," though the term will almost always be surrounded by a set of skeptical quotation marks. Gotta take your sociolinguistic jargon with a grain of salt, you know?

* A moment of silence for how phallic this word is.

possible—and sometimes inevitable—for the gender of a word to bleed into speakers' perceptions of what that word means.

In a language that assigns masculinity to the word *doctor* and femininity to the word *nurse*, its speakers might subconsciously start to think of those professions in a fundamentally gendered way. Grammar, Romaine argues, is a feminist concern, and there's a reason why suffixes and noun agreement have been at the center of the French feminist movement in a way that they haven't in the United States. That's because, in languages with grammatical gender, the sexist implications are out in the open, jumping up and down across every part of speech. In English, however, they're harder to catch. But in both types of languages, they can be overcome.

Why do some languages have grammatical gender in the first place? To answer that, let's rewind about a thousand years to a time when gender was only used to classify words, not people. The English word *gender* originally comes from the Latin *genus*, which means "kind" or "type," and in the beginning it was never applied to human beings. For centuries, masculine and feminine noun classes might as well just have been called "Thing 1" and "Thing 2"—they were seen as nothing but an effective way of structuring a language, and basically no one associated them with human sex. Way more languages had grammatical gender back then too, including English. Indeed, back in the days of Old English, we divided our

wordslut

nouns into masculine, feminine, and neuter classes, a structure that still exists in many Indo-European* languages today, like German, Greek, and Russian. It wasn't until that crazy William the Conqueror busted onto the English-speaking scene in 1066, bringing Old Norman French with him, that our three-way gender distinction died out, as did most of the suffixes distinguishing gender assignments. Eventually, English speakers decided that we didn't really need grammatical gender anymore, and we settled on the two-way "natural" gender system we have today.

It would still be a few hundred years before the word *gender* extended to describe people. And once it did, *sex* and *gender* were used interchangeably—we didn't have the body versus culture distinctions yet. Several centuries of overlapping meanings went by, and before you knew it, voilà: the grammatical sense of *gender* and the human senses got all messy and conflated.

Today, classifying every noun as masculine or feminine like they do in French and Spanish might seem overly complicated to most English speakers, but our natural gender system looks equally cumbersome to languages that don't have it. Hungarian, Finnish, Korean, Swahili, and Turkish are just a few of the world languages

---

* This is a huge family of several hundred languages ranging from Russia to Europe to the Middle East and parts of India. A language family is a group of related languages that descend from a common parent language. About 46 percent of the human population speaks an Indo-European language as their mother tongue, so you can think of English, Punjabi, Persian, and lots of others as distant cousins of the same great-great-great-grand-lingo.

that lack gendered pronouns like *he* and *she* entirely. How do you know who someone is talking about without naming their gender? Often it's just a matter of context, but some languages boast other creative gender-neutral solutions. The indigenous Algonquian languages of North America have two gender-nonspecific third-singular pronouns: Who gets which is determined by which person is more central to the conversation at hand. In these languages, your pronouns change depending on the topic you're discussing. This system is called *obviation*, and I think it's terribly clever.

Pronouns aside, there are also some languages that are essentially gender-free, containing very few words that make reference to a person's "natural" gender at all. Yoruba, a language spoken in Nigeria, has neither gendered pronouns nor the dozens of gendered nouns we have in English, including *son, daughter, host, hostess, hero, heroine*, etc. Instead, the most important distinction in Yoruba is the age of the person you're talking about. So, instead of saying brother and sister, you would say older sibling and younger sibling, or *egbun* and *aburo*. The only Yoruba words that make reference to a person's gender (or sex, as it were) are *obirin* and *okorin*, meaning "one who has a vagina" and "one who has a penis." So if you really wanted to call someone your sister, you would have to say *egbon mi obirin*, or "my older sibling, the one with the vagina." When you get that specific, it makes our English obsession with immediately identifying people's sexes seem just plain creepy.

wordslut

As a high school student, I took Italian as my foreign language (this is a language with grammatical gender), and while learning which words were feminine and masculine, I always wondered *how* exactly each noun got its gender assignment. Why were the words for table, chair, and fork feminine, while napkin, food, and knife were masculine? On the surface, it seemed totally random. But linguists agree that pairing nouns and genders is actually quite a complex process. Morphologist Greville G. Corbett once wrote that the rationale behind gender assignments varies considerably across languages. For some, the assignment is based on the sound or structure of the word; for others, it's based on the meaning; and for many, both the structure and the meaning are involved. Furthermore, it's very possible for a word's gender assignment (and the motivation for it) to shift over time.

Throughout history there have been a few male scholars who've tried to manipulate the relationship between grammatical gender and human gender to reflect their personal views of men and women. In the 1800s, a German grammarian named Jakob Grimm saw grammatical gender assignments as direct extensions of biological sex, a notion he deemed necessary for making sense of the world. "He spoke of the concept of grammatical gender as an extension of a 'natural' order onto each and every object," Romaine explains. "Things named by masculine nouns were, in Grimm's opinion, earlier, larger, firmer, quicker, more inflexible, active, moveable, creative; those which were feminine were later, smaller, softer, quieter, suffering/passive, receptive."

Grimm had a pal named Karl Lepsius, a linguist from Prussia, who agreed with this on-the-nose interpretation. Lepsius went so far as to claim that only the most civilized "leading nations in the history of mankind" distinguished between gendered nouns. To him, speakers of grammatically gendered languages had an overall more sophisticated understanding of the two human sexes. Languages without grammatical gender? They were "in decline."

As far as grammatical gender theory goes, Grimm and Lepsius were boneheads—if for no other reason than the fact that English seems to be doing pretty okay (oh, to have the confidence of a nineteenth-century Prussian man). And not everyone shares their extreme views about how "natural" gender should or shouldn't be reflected in language. Many scholars have actually decided that there is no connection, no "leakage," between them at all. But Grimm and Lepsius were right about one thing: grammatical gender and speakers' attitudes toward men and women are *not* always separate. They just aren't objective or inherently truthful either.

Sometimes they can be pretty darn sexist.

In languages with grammatical gender, there are entire ideas about men and women that cannot be communicated in a way that's "grammatically correct" by prescriptive standards. In French, for instance, most prestigious jobs are masculine: the French words for police officer, doctor, professor, engineer, politician, lawyer, surgeon, and dozens of others all have masculine gender. (The words for nurse, caretaker, and servant all happen to be feminine, though.) Thus, in French, if you wanted to say something like, "The doctor is brave," but the doctor is a woman and you want to indicate that, you're out of luck. Grammatically speaking, the noun *le docteur*, meaning doctor, and the adjective *courageux*, meaning brave, would both have to be masculine.

French feminists have tried to come up with alternatives— *la docteur, la docteure, la doctoresse*—but in France, there is a real-life grammar police, an official language council called the Académie française, which is reluctant to recognize such words or add them to the dictionary. (At the time I'm writing this only four of the current thirty-six members of the Académie are women. Yet somehow, six of the members are men named "Jean.")

In Italian, the masculine noun *segretario* refers to the prestigious position of a political secretary, like a secretary of state (a role traditionally held by men), while the feminine noun *segretaria* refers to a low-paid receptionist (a role traditionally held by women). Today, if a woman starts out as a *segretaria* in a government office and moves her way up to become a secretary to a politician, she would have to change the suffix of her title to a masculine one. For her, moving up professionally would literally mean having to masculinize her own title.

How much of an effect can these grammatical gender assignments truly have on the way people see the real world? A major one, and there's research to back this up. In 1962, scholars conducted an experiment where Italian speakers were presented with a series of made-up gibberish nouns that either ended in *o* or *a* (typically masculine and feminine suffixes in Italian, respectively). The speakers were asked to imagine what these faux nouns might represent and describe them using a list of adjectives: good, bad, strong, weak, small, large, etc. Then, they were asked to describe men and women using the same adjectives. The results? The feminine nouns, just like the women themselves, were described as good, weak, and small. The masculine nouns and men were bad, strong, and large. This study proves there's no way grammatical gender isn't leaking into speakers' worldviews.

There are also plenty of languages with noun classification systems that *aren't* explicitly gendered (and these speakers do not have a "lower consciousness" of the sexes, as Lepsius argued, whatever that even means). In the Tamil language of South India, nouns are divided by caste—either high caste or low caste. A Native American language called Ojibwa categorizes its nouns on the basis of "animate" or "inanimate" (which, to me, seems way more logical than the masculine-feminine distinction).

Tamil and Ojibwa are also examples of languages whose classification systems are not at all arbitrary but instead directly rely on what each word means (or meant at some point) to its speakers. People, animals, trees, and spirits belong to the animate class of Ojibwa nouns, but because of the speakers' cultural outlook, so do snow and cooking pots. Where cultural significance in noun classification starts to get problematic is when it happens in languages with masculine and feminine grammatical distinctions—there are several of these languages. Because grammatical gender and cultural perceptions of human gender are not separate for these speakers, theoretically, their impressions of men and women aren't able to escape the language's influence and would inevitably start to solidify as soon as they learn to talk.

One very untheoretical example of this comes from the Dyirbal language spoken in Aboriginal Australia. Dyirbal has four noun classes: the first is masculine, the second is feminine, the third is specifically for edible fruits and vegetables, and the fourth is for anything that doesn't fall into the first three. That might sound straightforward enough, but here's where it gets weird: an animal will always be assigned masculine gender in Dyirbal, unless it is notably more harmful or dangerous than the others in its category—in that case, it gets moved to the feminine class. For instance, while fish belong to the masculine category in Dyirbal, dangerous fish, like stonefish and garfish, are marked as feminine. So are all other potentially deadly creatures, as well as anything having to do with fire, water, or fighting. "The rationale for this categorization tells us something about how Dyirbal people conceive of their world and interact with it," Romaine says.

The Dyirbal system also serves as another example of treating masculine gender as the default. Sort of like, everything in the world of this language is male until given a good reason not to be. This default male pattern shows up in the grammar structures of hundreds of languages—in ways as understated as the French rule that only female nouns are marked with an *e*, or the fact that in Italian, a group of both male and female kids would automatically be called a group of "boys" (only when referring to a group of all girls would you use the feminine noun). Meanwhile, default maleness can be as overt as the Dizi language of Ethiopia, where almost every noun is classified as masculine, except for things singled out for being "naturally" female (girl, woman, cow), as well as things that are small in size (small broom, small pot). Ultimately, language can serve as a rather blatant means of otherizing all things feminine.

In Dyirbal's system, a noun is considered masculine unless it could literally kill you. This gender distinction between dangerous and nondangerous nouns might seem far-flung, but English speakers unwittingly do something similar. Think of all the instances where the pronoun *she* instead of *it* is used to refer to nonhuman things—namely, cars, boats, planes, oceans, countries, the Loch Ness monster, and hurricanes. (In the 1950s, the National Weather Service made the formal decision to assign solely female names to hurricanes, borrowing from naval meteorologists' tradition of naming their ships after women. Fortunately, in 1979 they got their gender equality act together and revised the system to include both male and female names.) All of these things are big, challenging, and have a long history of being conquered by men.

In 1995 United Airlines magazine printed an article titled "Boeing Beauty," penned by a pilot who described his Boeing 727 like this: "My wife JoAnna met her competition today. She has known about the 'other woman' for most of our 31 years of marriage . . . of course, I'm talking about an airplane . . . but what an airplane it is." A dad shows off his freshly waxed beamer—"Isn't she a beauty?" An IT guy stops by your desk at work to look at your malfunctioning laptop: "Open 'er up!" In 2011 a group of linguists published a study in the *Journal of Popular Culture* analyzing sexist souvenir T-shirts sold in the wake of Hurricane Katrina: slogans included "Katrina, That Bitch!"; "I Got Blown, Pissed On, and Fucked By Katrina: What a Whore"; and "Katrina Can Blow Me: She Won't Keep Me Away From Mardi Gras 2006."

In the 1920s male linguists came up with a name for this process of giving an object a human pronoun; they

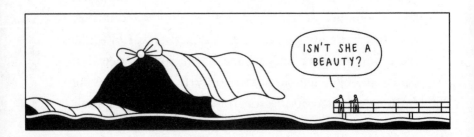

called it "upgrading," as if by calling these things "she," they are elevated to human status. They couldn't quite see that it simultaneously downgrades women to the status of toys and property.

In practice, what these metaphors of women as nature, territories, and technologies do is place feminine gender in that same distant category of "other." According to Romaine, by comparing her to things like storms and seas, "woman is symbolic of the conflict between nature and civilization, tempting men with her beauty, attracting men with her charms, but dangerous and therefore in need of conquest." Woman is a continent to colonize, a fortress to siege. These sentiments are reflected not only in English; in languages all over the world, from Italian to Thai, a nation's government is labeled as having "founding fathers," while the land itself ("Mother Nature," "virgin territory") is perceived as a feminine entity. In grammar as in allegory as in life, women are considered reckless places outside the civilized male world—wild things meant to be tamed into the weak, delicate flowers we've traditionally wanted women to be.

Some scholars believe that languages with grammatical gender have a more blatant impact on the attitudes of their speakers. A 1982 study suggested that children who grow up speaking a grammatically gendered language, like Hebrew, start to grasp their gender identities earlier than children who grow up speaking English or Finnish. One interpretation of these findings is that

wordslut

a language like Hebrew might be ideologically trapping its speakers into gender stereotypes sooner. But Romaine doesn't think of it that way. Because when a problem is more visible, it is often more discussed too. "In languages with grammatical gender, like French and Italian, speakers' attention is constantly drawn to the issue of gender in a way that it is not in a language like English," Romaine says. With more attention, a solution might be closer within reach.

In France especially, language is one of feminists' most powerful tools of resistance. French women often appropriate feminine-gendered terms in place of masculine ones, like using the feminine word *la personne*, meaning "person," instead of the masculine *le sujet*, to describe the subject of a story or conversation. "Although theoretically . . . [*le sujet*] supposedly encompasses both males and females, one of the tenets of French feminist theory is the argument that patriarchy constructs the subject as masculine and effectively excludes women," Romaine explains. "Paradoxically, its apparent grammatical inclusion of women guarantees their exclusion."

In English, we've introduced the more inclusive term *person* as a substitute for *man* in words like *chairperson* and *salesperson*—but the difference is that while English attempts to remove gender from the word entirely, the French *la personne* is explicitly feminine. English *person* doesn't make the same dramatic statement, as it doesn't actively shift the position of the subject to feminine soil. "The political significance of the use of *personne* by French women is lost when translated into English," comments Romaine. And while it is possible for feminists to draw attention to the English language in a similar way—it's often done through wordplay and respellings, like *herstory, womyn,* and *shero*—it just doesn't seem to gain as much traction.

Part of that might be because not everyone is cool with "feminizing" words that are already technically gender neutral. Many women comedians have said they detest when people call them *comediennes.* "I don't like it," *Broad City* star Ilana Glazer told *Elle* magazine in 2016. "Do they call them doctresses?" Margaret Cho agreed: "I like stand-up comic better. Just comic."

Psycholinguistic studies show that in English, excessively "girly" suffixes like *-ette* and *-ess* possess actively negative or at least diminutive connotations. After all, *-ette* did not start out as a feminine suffix, but as a way to refer to something smaller or of lesser value (*kitchenette, cigarette*). Words like *actress* and *waitress* are still in everyday use, but there used to be way more of these gendered nouns: *neighboress, singeress, servantess, spousess, friendess, farmeress,* and indeed *doctoress* were all real words in Middle English that have faded into obscurity.

Many women object to these feminized suffixes, but others adore them: just like some women actively like their gender to be highlighted in phrases such as "female writer" or "woman scientist," there are women who delight in and identify with explicitly "girly" grammatical

wordslut

structures. Not long ago, I posted on social media that the Italian language distinguishes between male and female elephants—*elefante* means "boy elephant;" *elefantessa* means "girl elephant"—and while half of the comments I received expressed that this seemed odd and gratuitous, I also got several messages from women who thought the *-essa* suffix was enchantingly femme and not belittling at all.

Plenty of women find charm in feminine suffixes. A UK organization encouraging young girls to pursue science, technology, engineering, and math boasts the company name STEMette. I recently came across the website of a female business owner who calls herself an "entrepreneuress." There's no conclusive right answer to whether or not these words are sexist. But it is worth thinking about why we perceive them the way we do.

Women are certainly not the only people who benefit from critiquing grammatical gender—it is both politically meaningful, and just plain practical, for trans and gender-nonconforming folks too. You might think that a person who doesn't identify as either a man or a woman would be screwed in a language like French, but queer speakers are coming up with some pretty creative ways to solve these problems. "People can actually use a binary grammatical gender system to position themselves outside of that binary," says Santa Barbara linguist Lal Zimman, who leads workshops for schoolteachers on how to give gender-inclusive instruction in languages with binary systems.

Queer speakers of Hebrew, for example, often use a mixture of masculine and feminine forms, or invent entirely new ones, to express their queer identities in ways that English speakers don't have the opportunity to. In 2016 news circulated about a Hebrew-speaking summer camp in Maryland that allows kids to modify gendered suffixes so that everyone can feel included. In Hebrew, like in Italian, you would use the masculine term for "kids" to describe any group that contains at least one boy. The Hebrew word for "kids" ends in the masculine suffix *-im*—the feminine version of the word ends in the suffix *-ot*—but at Camp Moshova, groups of both boys and girls use a mix of the two: the newly invented suffix *-imot*. Even the word for *camper* is gendered in Hebrew—*chanich* means male camper, and *chanichah* means female camper—leaving out any folks who don't think of themselves as either. At camp, however, a nonbinary kid can use a new, gender-neutral form of the word: *chanichol*.

Sociolinguists tend to think of these new language usages as fascinating and exciting, but not everyone is quite as pumped. Many people I know (or see on Reddit)—people who *never* think or care about "proper grammar" in their everyday lives—suddenly get very unsettled at the idea of someone changing a word just because they want to. Grammar, as they see it, is a supreme, stable authority that you shouldn't be able to challenge so freely.

In the United States, a lot of this drama has to do with pronouns. As transgender and nonbinary identities

wordslut

become more and more visible, so does the discussion of "preferred pronouns,"* and many people who identify as neither male nor female are choosing to go by singular *they*. But not everyone is on board yet. Folks often defend their resistance to using *they* to describe one person by arguing that the word as they learned it is plural; using it any other way, they contest, would be grammatically incorrect.

There are two huge flaws in their logic: The first is that using a plural pronoun for a singular meaning is nothing new for English speakers. A few hundred years ago, the second-person *you* was exclusively a plural; *thou* was the singular version (e.g., "Thou shalt not kill," "Thou shalt not lie"). Eventually, *you* extended to the singular meaning and pushed out *thou* entirely. Who's to say the same thing couldn't happen with *they*?

The other key defect in the argument against singular *they* is that most people already use it so naturally that they don't even realize they're doing it. (I've used singular *they* once in this chapter so far—100 points to anyone who finds it.) English speakers have been using *they* as a singular pronoun to refer to someone whose gender is unknown to them ever since the days of Middle English ("Someone left *their* goblet in the gatehouse"). If we're

---

* I put "preferred pronouns" in quotes because many nonbinary folks see it as a misnomer. The argument is that pronouns aren't preferred or unpreferred—they're either correct or incorrect. To a nonbinary person, being referred to with a gendered pronoun would be just as inaccurate as someone using the word *he* to describe my mom. It's not a preference thing; it's an accuracy thing.

talking grammar rules, singular *they* was considered perfectly acceptable as a generic third-singular pronoun all the way up until the late eighteenth century. That's when grammarians decided that people should start using generic *he* instead. Their reasoning? That's what they used to do in Latin. (English speakers' obsession with Latin has inspired a great many of our most confusing grammar rules, like when to use "you and I" versus "you and me.") Consequently, style books adopted generic *he*, as did most educators, who quickly convinced themselves that singular *they*, in any context, was not only grammatically unacceptable but fundamentally "illogical."

And yet, millions of everyday people, including plenty of respected writers, ignored the new generic *he* rule and continued using *they* as a gender-nonspecific pronoun anyway. Jane Austen was all about singular *they* and used it precisely seventy-five times throughout her six novels. (Check out this line from *Pride and Prejudice*: "But to expose the former faults of any person, without knowing what their present feelings were, seemed unjustifiable.") Add to that all the protests from second-wave feminists who contested that generic *he* was sexist, and eventually, grammar authorities listened. Today, many reputable grammar sources, like the *AP Stylebook*, formally endorse singular *they*, as do influential institutions from Facebook to the government of Canada. Because ultimately, most people agreed that in practical usage, generic *they* simply works better than generic *he*, no matter what the books said.

wordslut

These days, the only problem anyone seems to have with singular *they* is when they're specifically being asked to use it because someone doesn't identify as either *he* or *she*. This is when you start hearing arguments about how it defies basic grammar rules and is just too confusing to bother with. I personally know a few people who've argued that if we just came up with a brand-new pronoun, that would solve the whole problem, because then at least you'd always know the speaker was referring to one person, as opposed to multiple. The issue there is that we already tried that, and it didn't work. Twenty years ago, *they* was not the most common nonbinary pronoun used in genderqueer communities—instead, it was the gender-neutral singular pronoun *ze* (pronounced like the letter *z*). If singular *they* has had it tough, *ze* was up against a mountain of pushback. Learning a new word altogether was harder for most English speakers to accept than simply starting to use a word that already exists in a slightly new context, which is all that singular *they* requires. (Though there is at least one language in modern history where introducing an entirely new pronoun worked. In July 2014 the Swedish gender-neutral third-singular pronoun *hen* was added to the official dictionary next to *han* and *hon*, meaning *he* and *she*. Many people adopted *hen* into their vocabularies with little complaint.)

I will admit, while it can be difficult to adjust to using *they* when referring to a specific person, like any new skill, it takes practice, and most people don't mind if you make an honest mistake. I've certainly made my fair share of slipups learning how to use singular *they*. But the blunders were genuine, no one got upset, and now singular *they* comes quite naturally.

For anyone else who would like to step up their pronoun game but is still a little confused, Lal Zimman has an amazing tip: think of people's pronouns just like you think of their names. You can't tell a person's name just by looking at them; if you want to know it, you have to ask, and to argue with their answer would be weird and rude. Everyone has their own individual name, and it may be difficult to remember or pronounce, but it is common courtesy to try your best to learn it. (Just as it would be unreasonable to say, "What? Your name is Chrysanthemum? No, that's too much for me, I think I'll call you Bob," it would be equally bananas to use a pronoun that someone explicitly told you wasn't theirs.) People are also allowed to change their names whenever they want—if we mess up the new one occasionally, that's fine, but eventually, everyone just has to accept it, or, again, it would be weird and rude. Indeed, twenty years from now, introducing yourself with your name *and* your pronouns could become the norm. "Hi, my name is Amanda, she/her—you?" "I'm Sam, they/them. Nice to meet you." Is that really so mind-boggling?

To some people that does seem mind-boggling. But for those who outright refuse to learn new pronouns, grammar does not work as a defense, because language

wordslut

scholars know that isn't really the problem. If you don't approve of nonbinary identity or feel the need to affirm it, then it's possible to find a reason to avoid using gender-neutral language no matter what. "This is one of those things where people start with a conclusion and work backward to find an argument," Lal Zimman says, before telling me a story about how his partner, who uses they/them pronouns, is always butting heads with their mother, who can't be convinced to get on board. "And their mom constantly just asserts 'It's because *they* is plural for me. It would be so much easier if you just used *ze*.' And so, eventually my partner was just like, 'Okay, use *ze* then, if that's really gonna be easier for you,' and that hasn't improved her accuracy at all."

It makes sense that these structural linguistic changes cause such strong reactions. This isn't just an issue of gendered pronouns, either: long before nonbinary identity and singular *they* were a part of the mainstream cultural dialogue, meeting certain grammatical standards was still highly valued by English speakers. It has been for centuries—and historically, this hasn't had much to do with gender at all. Instead, it has to do with money and social class.

See, during Europe's feudal period—the time of lords, ladies, and peasants—if you were born poor, you'd stay poor forever. In those days, learning to talk "properly" was not a thing, because it would be useless. It wouldn't change anything about your life. But with the end of feudalism in the fifteenth century came new opportunities for class mobility. That's also around the time the printing press was invented, and with it came the publication of grammatical guides. Now that there was a chance you could possibly become a member of a higher social class, people began to take an interest in learning how to talk like one. Soon, a "standard" form of language was agreed upon by the state and the education system, which reinforced this linguistic hierarchy. Over the centuries, the importance of ascending that hierarchy became more and more culturally embedded.

In the United States, a mastery of English grammar has become tied to the American dream itself. A friend of mine, who is first-generation American, once told me that when she was growing up, her Japanese father made her put a dollar in a jar every time she used a slang word. "He thought it made me sound low class," she said. "He was an immigrant." For folks like my friend's dad, speaking "proper" English is the way to the big house with the white picket fence. It's the idea that if you want to be a CEO, you have to sound like one, and not caring about grammar means not caring about your future itself.

All that said, it's also true that not all language purists have the same background or whip out their red pen with the same agenda in mind. Plenty of folks oppose singular *they* due to their social conservatism, but some of the biggest grammar snobs in America actually come from the political left. Deborah Cameron has said that one of the first things she noticed upon joining Twitter in 2014 was how often educated progressive types called upon their

wordslut

superior grammar skills to confront bigots. Take a look at this Twitter exchange from 2016:

> A: *As a straight male how would u feel about yr child having a homosexual school teacher?! Who their around for 8hrs of the day?*
> B: *If a gay teacher teaches my child the difference between they're, their and there, I'm good.*

In a world of highly divided politics, most of which are voiced online, grammar-based digs like the one in this tweet* have become some of the first projectiles launched to confront racist, homophobic, and xenophobic remarks. A 2016 news story out of the United Kingdom told of a white woman verbally accosting an immigrant woman, who responded to the harassment by saying, "I speak better English than you!" The victim later told reporters that the bigot's "grammar was appalling."

You can't blame someone in this situation for defending themselves however they can—but you have to ask why claiming to have better grammar than your antagonist is so often the weapon of choice. Linguists posit that this has to do with notion that bigots are not only depraved, but also stupid, and that the two are connected. "It allows their critics to feel intellectually and culturally

---

* For the record, messing up they're/their/there or your/you're/yore would technically be an issue of *spelling*, not grammar . . . but it's pedantry all the same.

as well as morally superior," Cameron explains. That is a satisfying feeling, to be sure, but the reality is that grammar and morality don't actually have anything to do with one another, and attacking a bigot's poor grammar does not itself prove you are a better person. It might prove that you had the opportunity to become more educated than they did, or that you spent a lot of time mastering the rules of standard English. However, the moral significance of what someone says is about the content, not the grammar. As Cameron says, "Hitler wasn't any less fascist because he could write a coherent sentence."

The other problem with policing people's preposition usage or dangling modifiers is that "poor grammar" is often a criticism hurled at what is really just a nonstandard English dialect. For instance, one might call out a speaker of African-American Vernacular English (AAVE) for using a double negative ("I didn't say nothing") without realizing that AAVE is a systematic dialect, and the double negative isn't a mistake but instead a legitimate part of AAVE grammar. It isn't something we find in standard English anymore, but it used to be—centuries ago, everyone from Chaucer to Shakespeare to everyday English speakers used double negatives. Again, it wasn't until those stuffy grammarians from the English standardization period decided we should copy Latin and nix the double negative that it was considered "incorrect."

Linguists know that nonstandard forms of a language are not objectively "bad." The grammatical forms them-

wordslut

selves, like saying "he be"* instead of "he is," are not inherently worse or better than what we learned in English class. They're simply stigmatized based on how we feel about the type of person using them.

When highly educated folks engage in grammar policing, they're basically just doing what misogynists do when they dismiss what a woman is saying because she uses uptalk or vocal fry; it's another example of judging someone's speech based on preconceptions of who they are. Discerning listeners can tell that addressing someone's grammar is often just a way of avoiding the message itself. "Language pedantry is snobbery and snobbery is prejudice," Cameron says. "And that, IMHO, is nothing to be proud of."

There's something that all of these grammar critics— from the opposers of singular *they*, to the grammar-splainers on Twitter, to France's Académie française—have in common. Whatever their political beliefs, they all possess a profound urge to correct or halt change in speech. This is true of most people. Whenever language

---

* In AAVE, phrases like "he be singing" and "he be eating" feature a unique grammatical tense called "habitual be." A common misconception is that AAVE speakers arbitrarily use *be* instead of *is* in every situation, but the two actually mean something different. Habitual *be* is used to mark a repeated or customary action, so while a sentence like "He is singing" would mean "he is *currently* singing," the sentence "He be singing" would mean he is someone who sings all the time. In a famous 2005 experiment, young speakers of both standard English and AAVE were shown images of Elmo eating cookies while Cookie Monster watched. Both sets of kids agreed that Elmo *is* eating cookies, but the AAVE speakers said that Cookie Monster *be* eating cookies, because that's a known habit of his character.

changes, as when anything in life changes, folks can't help but feel a little fussy. That's because language change is frequently a sign of bigger social changes, which makes people anxious. It's why people above the age of forty have always loathed teen slang, no matter the era: it represents a new generation rising up and taking over. One of my mom's friends, a guy in his late fifties, recently told me he "hates" so many of today's popular slang words (*shade, lit, G.O.A.T.*) because "they do nothing to improve the English language." What's funny is that I can almost promise, forty years ago, his parents were saying the exact same thing about *cool, bummer,* and *freaking out,* all phrases that have now taken a seat at the table of acceptable English terminology but started out as annoying teen slang.

The type of language change that's gotten perhaps the worst reputation is the push toward political correctness. The conservative media has played a big role in painting this concept as a negative, in propagating the idea that in this day and age "you can't say anything anymore." The fear is that being forced to use gender-inclusive language, like singular *they, Mx. instead of Mrs. and Mr.,* and *friends* instead of "boys and girls," poses a threat to free speech.

In reality, of course, no one can *force* anyone to say anything in this country—political correctness does not endanger our freedom of expression at all. The only thing it actually threatens is the notion that we can separate our word choices from our politics—that how we

wordslut

choose to communicate doesn't say something deeper about who we are. As American English speakers, we are perfectly at liberty to use whatever language we want; we just have to know that our words reveal our social and moral beliefs to some extent. So if one were to use the term *comedienne* instead of *comic* or the pronoun *she* to describe a Ferrari, they could be opening themselves up to criticism, not for flat-out sexism but definitely for expressing an indifference to gender equality. What rubs people the wrong way about political correctness is not that they can't use certain words anymore, it's that political neutrality is no longer an option.

In defense of their objection to linguistic change, some folks will claim that their "brain just doesn't work that way." They simply "can't handle" new rules like gender-neutral pronouns. To that, my answer is this: How about we set up the next generation to have brains that can? "What we really need is to change the way we teach language early in life," says Lal Zimman. If we considered the ability to easily change the pronoun you use to refer to somebody as a valuable skill, that could be a part of our language arts education. We could incorporate all kinds of gender-inclusive language instruction into our grammar lessons. After all, there's no reason acquiring linguistic flexibility shouldn't be as appreciated as being able to know when to use *well* versus *good* or *your* versus *you're*.

In the meantime, we can either do our best to get on

board or not—but whatever we choose, we can trust that language will move along its merry way regardless. The bigots and the pedants will be left at the station, and a generation of linguistically bendy, gender-inclusive whizzes will ride off into the sunset.

I hope to see you there. I hear it'll be quite the party.

how to confuse a catcaller

(and other ways to verbally smash the patriarchy)

In India, they call it *Eve teasing*, which I think is quite poetic. I picture earth's first man tiptoeing friskily behind earth's first woman, his fig leaf fluttering in the breeze. In Syria, it's sometimes called *taltish*, which isn't as innocent. This word, with its harsh pair of letter *t*'s, describes a brisk way of saying something, as if tossed upon the hearer, like a martini to the face. *Piropos* are famous throughout Latin America: the term comes from the Ancient Greek *pyropus*, which means "fire-colored." It is said that Romans appropriated this word to mean "red-colored precious stones," similar to rubies, which represented the heart, and hence were the stones men gave to the women they were courting. (Those who didn't have money for these gems gave them pretty words instead.) But the only term I've ever used to describe it was invented in eighteenth-century England. There, it referred to the act of heckling vulnerable theater performers: "Nice costume, dandy!"; "Get off the stage!" In English, we call it *catcalling*.

So many languages offer a phrase to describe the act of a person (usually a man) shouting sexual comments in the street at someone they don't know (usually a woman or feminine-presenting person), because in almost every country, you are sure to find it. As much as catcallers claim that their behavior is meant to be flattering ("Where are you going, baby?"; "Damn, look at that ass!"), both social scientists and people who deal with catcalling firsthand can tell that's not really the intent. As a college student, an age when I would have been thrilled for just about anybody to think I was sexy, I was catcalled wearing everything from a minidress and heels to a matching Halloween pajama set from Duane Reade. The shirt said "Boo!" and so did the catcaller, before asking for my hand in marriage.

That guy didn't want to marry me or even make me feel good about myself, but he did want me to hear him and to understand that he had control over me, at least for those few seconds. Because the act of catcalling isn't really about sex—it's about power.

Since the beginning of patriarchy, language has been

a primary means through which men have asserted their dominance in order to make sure women and other oppressed genders have no control over what happens to them. And though salaciously taunting strangers in public may be one of the flashiest tactics, it's hardly the only one. Equally disempowering are the practices of labeling women *overemotional, hormonal, crazy,* or *hysterical** as a way to discredit their experiences, or addressing female colleagues as *sweetheart* or *young lady* in a professional setting as a form of (often subconscious) subordination. I once worked in an office where the company's owner referred to every female employee by her hair color: "You're early today, blondie." "How's that write-up coming, pink?" (We worked alongside a male employee with a zigzag design shaved into the back of his head, but the boss just called him Daniel.)

Other gender-based power plays include speaking to women in a patronizingly "teachy" manner, aka *mansplaining.* One of the most blatant examples of mansplaining from recent memory comes from a video that went viral in 2017 of a physics panel featuring six brilliant

* The word *hysteria* has been gendered for millennia. Derived from the Ancient Greek word for *womb,* by the nineteenth century it had evolved to describe a "female mental disorder" characterized by emotional instability without cause. It is theorized that a common treatment for hysteria during that time was something called "hysterical paroxysm," which involved a male doctor masturbating a female patient to orgasm. Today, mental health experts thankfully understand that hysteria is not a real disorder. And yet the word *hysterical* remains, a ghost from a time when if you were a woman with a legitimate illness, you could expect to have a doctor invalidate you, then diddle you, and think that was all quite normal and good. Which is enough to make a person go truly crazy.

wordslut

scientists, one of whom was a woman, UC Davis professor Veronika Hubeny. An hour into the discussion, the male moderator (not a physicist) finally directed a question at Hubeny, only to begin immediately talking over her, trying and failing to explain her research himself. It took an audience member shouting, "Let her speak, please!" prompting the audience to erupt in applause, for the moderator, at long last, to zip his flap.

Consistently interrupting women as they're speaking is a similar ploy for control. Much research has shown that women are routinely interrupted more than men, both at work and in social scenarios (a small but significant 1975 survey found that men were responsible for almost 98 percent of the interruptions recorded in mixed-sex conversations). Worse yet, there's also the act of not responding at all. Robin Lakoff once pointed out that while interrupting someone frustratingly tells them that they have no right to the floor, or that what they're saying isn't important, nonresponse renders the victim's speaking status nonexistent to begin with. As if to say, the idea of a woman making a worthwhile contribution is so meaningless that as far as the listener is concerned, her statement might as well just have been a loud gust of wind and therefore does not merit a response. I remember once pitching a project to a group of creative higher-ups, the boss of whom was a British guy in his sixties—he didn't say a word for the entire meeting, and when I was finished, he immediately picked up the conversation he was having with his colleague before I got there, as if the last forty-five minutes had simply . . . never happened.

And then there's the act of dismissing a woman's testimony when she comes forward with any of these offenses.

Pointing out that men use language to dominate women both regularly and casually is not exactly news. It's hard to forget that until relatively recently, women were not even considered people in a legal or political sense (American women weren't able to own property until the late 1800s or vote until half a century later, and that was just white ladies). Even as women become incrementally better represented in business and government, things don't naturally get better for them as a whole. Instead, it's often true that as women gain more freedom and control, men's use of these linguistic power moves increases accordingly. Because men have gotten so used to speaking for everyone, thanks to millennia of doing so, when women begin to creep into their territory, they feel as though they have to do something to reassert the authority they've been taught for so long is rightfully theirs. In a way, catcalling, interruption, disregarding a woman by telling her she's crazy, and other forms of silencing are in response to this gradual challenging of the power scales. It's all a way of rendering what women think and say irrelevant, a justification for keeping them from the authority they've begun to reclaim.

"Silencing is always political," Robin Lakoff said in a 1992 paper. "To be voiceless is to have no 'say' in what gets done, what happens to one, to have no representation. . . . To be deprived of speech is to be deprived of humanity itself—in one's own eyes and in the eyes of others." When one's humanity is taken away, the obligation to treat them equally is also removed. "So the silencing of women, in all its forms, is more than a convenience allowing men to enjoy conversation more," Lakoff said. "It is the basic tool by which political inequity is created, reinforced, and made to seem inevitable."

The hopeful truth is that inequity is not *actually* inevitable. To correct it, what we need is to convince the people who currently have a monopoly on the microphone—and thus a monopoly on social and political control itself—to do as our preschool teachers told us and let someone else have a turn. What we also need is to empower those who have been convinced that they don't deserve access to the microphone to seize it firsthand. The tricky part is that none of that can happen until we're able to grasp why these acts of linguistic domination happen the way they do—we have to understand the social functions of catcalling, interruption, and other forms of gender-based verbal harassment. This understanding will help us see why our current strategies for dealing with linguistic power moves haven't worked very well so far, and ultimately, what we can do better.

In recent history, acts of verbal dominance have gotten worse, not better. A 2017 study analyzing Supreme Court oral argument transcripts from 1990, 2002, and 2015 determined that as more female justices were added to the bench, interruptions of women did not improve but escalated. Using the logic that more female justices would normalize female power, you might expect the opposite result. "Interruptions are attempts at dominance . . . so the more powerful a woman becomes, the less often she should be interrupted," the researchers wrote. Instead, they found that in 1990, when Justice Sandra Day O'Connor was the only woman on the bench, 35.7 percent of overall interruptions were aimed at her (which, out of nine justices, was already a high percentage); twelve years later, after Ruth Bader Ginsburg was added, 45.3 percent were directed at the two female justices; and in 2015, with three women on the bench (Ginsburg, Sonia Sotomayor, and Elena Kagan), 65.9 percent of all court interruptions on the court were aimed at female justices.

"With more women on the court, the situation only seems to be getting worse," wrote the study's authors, who were also able to prove that the motivation for interruption definitely had to do with gender, as opposed to experience on the bench. This confirmation came after finding that female justices more than males were persistently cut off not only by their male colleagues but also by their male subordinates—the advocates on the floor attempting to persuade them. "Even though Supreme Court justices are some of the most powerful individuals in the country [with interruption], gender is approximately 30 times more powerful than seniority," the authors concluded. (Not to mention, in 2015, the most common type of interruption of any individual justice was by male advocates speaking over Justice Sotomayor—this dynamic accounted for 8 percent of all of the court's interruptions. Sotomayor is also the only female Supreme Court justice of color.)

Most women haven't experienced being interrupted on the Supreme Court bench, but they have experienced catcalling. Out of all the linguistic methods used to subordinate women, we tend to hear a lot about street harassment because (a) it is the one form of gendered subjugation that nearly everyone who's ever been female (or perceived as female) has been put through, and (b) almost everyone who has absolutely hates it. According to a pair of 2014 surveys from nonprofit organizations Hollaback! and Stop Street Harassment, somewhere between 65 percent and 85 percent of all American women experience catcalling by age seventeen. Recipients include women of all ages, races, income levels, sexual orientations, and geographic locations, as well as many men, especially men who aren't straight or cisgender. The Stop Street Harassment numbers showed that respondents who identified as lesbian, gay, bisexual, or transgender were significantly more likely to experience street harassment than anyone else. Black and Hispanic respondents were at greater risk too.

In an episode of *This American Life*, Australian journalist Eleanor Gordon-Smith attempted to interview every man who catcalled her on a busy street in Sydney. To persuade one of the men she confronted that women do not in fact enjoy unwelcome sexual commentary from strangers, she quoted a poll stating that 67 percent of women think that an interaction with a catcaller is going to become violent. Eighty-five percent feel angry after being catcalled, 78 percent feel annoyed, 80 percent feel nervous, and 72 percent feel disgusted. In 2017 I conducted a small survey of my own, asking my friends on social media to tell me how catcalling made them feel in one word: *small*, *degraded*, and *objectified* were among the top responses. According to Hollaback!, only 3 percent of women find catcalling flattering.

This 3 percent number is especially interesting when you consider the fact that most men accused of sexual harassment say that they're simply shelling out appreciation. "I didn't mean anything by it," "It's just a compliment," and "We're just ordinary people. We want to say hi," are a few of the responses linguists have collected from confronted catcallers. Statistics aside, one of the biggest flaws of these defenses is that whistling at someone you don't know as they walk by, offering unsolicited appraisals of their outfit or demeanor, and commenting on body parts not normally available for public scrutiny violate pretty much every norm of compliment behavior experts have identified. (The most pertinent of these behavioral observations, according to a 2008 analysis, is that the majority of men's compliments to women have nothing at all to do with appearance but instead with softening face-threatening acts such as requests or criticism. And they almost always occur between people who know each other, e.g., "Kate, you know you're my favorite, but can you please try to show up on time tomorrow?"). In a 2009 paper titled "The compliment as a social strategy," linguists Nessa Wolfson and Joan Manes determined that whatever the immediate discourse function, "complimenting has the underlying social function of creating or reinforcing solidarity between the speaker and the addressee." If asked to illustrate the concept of bonding via flattery to an alien race unfamiliar with human social interaction, I think we can all agree that "Smile!" and "Let me tap that ass" would not be considered good examples.

In 2017 comedian Peter White put the lunacy of the compliment argument into perspective with this pithy statement: "I think the golden rule for men should be: If you're a man, don't say anything to a woman on the street that you wouldn't want a man saying to you in prison."

Objectively, having your body spontaneously critiqued by a stranger in the street is so bizarrely unlike any other human-to-human encounter that it's genuinely impossible to know how to respond. For all of my teenage years, catcalling distressed me so much that whenever it happened, I simply kept my head down and didn't react. But in my early twenties, after having tickled my inner revolutionary with the teachings of a gender and language class or two, I decided to try my hand at confronting them. Because I'd heard that many men who do this are just looking for a quick reaction, and that a smile or the flick of a middle finger were considered equal successes, I tried to give my catcallers something less expected.

"I know why you're doing this," I said once to a pair of boys in backward caps, who'd hollered that they'd like to "show me a good time" in Union Square Park. "You're trying to prove how straight you are to each other. I've studied people like you in school. You can't fool me." I highly doubt I convinced any of the men I confronted to stop catcalling forever, but I did bamboozle and embarrass a few of them, and those felt like small victories in the moment. I remember one guy actually ran away from me. I'm sure it was because he felt annoyed rather than defeated, but it did the trick.

On social media I asked my friends to tell me their personal favorite techniques for coping with catcallers and was inundated with responses: among them were shouting in a foreign language to freak them out, making ugly faces to confuse them, and staring them down to make them feel uncomfortably seen. I even asked Deborah Cameron what she's done in the face of street harassment: "I've told them to fuck off on occasion," she told me, "but like most women I'm wary of getting into it with them—it's potentially dangerous."*

Unfortunately, Cameron thinks that spending any more time on a catcaller—attempting to reason with them or change their behavior—is likely a waste of time. "They aren't listening, especially if they're in a group," she said. "Hypothetically, it might be interesting to just say to a catcaller, 'Can you explain to me why you just said that?' and keep questioning every answer, and watch him struggle to make any sense of his own behavior. But I can't really see your average street harasser sticking around for that kind of interview."

Even when they do, the results aren't exactly promising. On Gordon-Smith's episode of *This American Life*, she was able to persuade only one of her dozens of catcallers to stop and have a real conversation with her. A former speech and debate competitor, Gordon-Smith gave the guy every rational argument to reconsider his behavior: statistics, insightful questions, emotionally charged personal anecdotes. But in the end, he just couldn't be convinced.

---

* It's true, most people I spoke with agree that ignoring the catcalls—not giving these speakers the time of day—feels like the smartest move. "My most effective strategy has always been to pretend I am so consumed by everything else going on around me that I don't even hear or notice the catcaller," a twenty-four-year-old from Atlanta, Georgia, told me in an Instagram message. "I get the sense that this makes them feel small, which is how being catcalled makes me feel . . . so HA!"

After 120 minutes with this man—whom she described as otherwise sweet, friendly, and "not a bad guy"—the only thing Gordon-Smith was able to accomplish was getting him to promise to no longer physically attack women in the street (he was big into ass slapping). Discontinuing his verbal comments was something he did not feel compelled to do (which he couldn't come up with a particularly cogent reason for). "Compliments, when I feel they're appropriate . . . I think I'm still gonna do," he said, after which Gordon-Smith argued that she still felt he was choosing his fun over women's feelings. Said the guy: "Well, that's kinda just the selfishness of the world."

Gordon-Smith made one last point: "Can I tell you why I found this stuff really depressing?" she asked. "I feel like I've been walking around for days now believing that people want to be nice, and believing that it comes from a good place, and believing that guys are just trying to have fun and compliment people. But it's real, real hard for me to keep believing that when I tell people how angry it makes us, I tell people how sad it makes us, I tell people about sexual violence statistics, and the reaction isn't, 'That matters to me, and I'm going to stop.' The reaction is, 'That doesn't matter to me.'"

The unfortunate truth is that Gordon-Smith was right: simply informing a catcaller or any other verbal harasser that his words are hurtful is not enough to make him stop. And this isn't because the person is a bad apple. If only it were that simple. Instead, it's because of a much

wordslut

larger problem with what dudes in our culture believe belongs to them.

The fundamental reason why street harassment sucks is the same reason why a male coworker calling a female coworker "sweetheart" sucks, which is the same reason why it sucks when a man touches a woman he doesn't know in a way he would never touch a man (like by placing his hands on her hips as he slides past her in a crowded bar). The underlying problem with all of these forms of sexual trespassing is that they rely on the assumption that a man has an automatic right to a woman's body. It's a display of social control, signaling to women that they are intruders in a world owned by men, and thus have no right to privacy.

When a man touches or says intimate things to a woman he doesn't know, there is an implication that he has an inherent access to the recipient's sexuality, which reduces her to a plaything and draws the focus away from any of her more relevant or impressive identities. Scholar Beth A. Quinn once pointed out that according to research on sexual assault, calling attention to a woman's sexuality can function "to exclude recognition of her competence, rationality, trustworthiness, and even humanity." In other words, a woman could be a CEO of a company, have an IQ of 180, or be a prosecutor making her case in a courtroom, but the second the male defense attorney calls her "honey,"* all of that is

---

* Thankfully, using sexist remarks like this in the courtroom was banned by the American Bar Association in 2016. (In Canada, lawyers are

taken away. (By contrast, a man calling attention to his own (hetero)sexuality—which catcalling also does— actually makes him seem *more* worthy of respect. As Quinn says, "The power of sexuality is asymmetrical, in part, because being seen as sexual has different consequences for women and men.")

This expression of overfamiliarity is not something that happens only to women, by the way. Our culture has a worrisome habit of treating all kinds of marginalized groups—people of color, queer folks, people of lower socioeconomic class—with a presumptuous level of intimacy. A 2017 study of body-camera footage revealed that police officers were 61 percent more likely to use low-respect language, such as informal titles like "my man," with black drivers than they were with white drivers. Interactions like this are not a sign of affection or something the recipient should be flattered by. Because really, they're just a signal that the speaker considers them of inferior status and has some sort of preapproved license signed by the universe to treat them as such.

There is one unified reason why many men feel as though they have an inherent right to comment on women's bodies, ignore them in meetings, or dismiss them with the excuse that they're on their periods and acting hysterical: it's because of a lack of *empathy*. Studies of sexual harassers show that when a woman retaliates against a man's sexual trespassing (which she's not

required to address one another with stock gender-neutral phrases like "my learned friend," which I think is a charming solution.)

supposed to do, of course, because she's just an object to him) and is by some miracle believed and the dude is confronted, he will likely make some excuse about his intentions. He'll say that he was misinterpreted and meant no harm. He'll say that he's a "good guy" and that he doesn't deserve to be complained about or have his reputation tarnished for a little playful repartee.

But when he says this stuff, he's really just playing dumb. Because research shows that when sexual harassers are asked to switch places with their targets, they are able to grasp quite quickly that what they've done is wrong. It's not that their intentions have been misunderstood— these dudes realize the harm they've caused. It's simply that they aren't motivated to care. They lack empathy. And this, underneath it all, has to do with a problem of how our culture teaches men to be men.

Our standards of masculinity are extreme and undue: they require that men be powerful, exhaustingly heterosexual, and utterly unrelated to femininity at all costs. In order to perform and protect that masculine identity, men quickly learn that in many cases, they must mask a woman's viewpoint and disregard her pain. As Beth A. Quinn wrote in 2002, "Men fail to exhibit empathy with women because masculinity precludes them from taking the position of the feminine other, and men's moral stance vis-à-vis women is attenuated by this lack of empathy." This empathy deficit toward all things feminine surely hurts men too, as the masculinity standards that cause it do not allow men to display any emotional, physical, or linguistic characteristics that could possibly be construed as womanlike. So they often lock themselves up in a rigid box of heteronormative masculine behavior out of fear that being perceived as feminine will endanger them and take their power away.

I think this empathy issue is also part of what's going on with interruption, nonresponse, mansplaining, calling women "hysterical," and many of the other linguistic power moves we've identified so far. Because masculinity as we know it discourages men from forming solidarity with women, when a dude ignores or strong-arms a woman's voice, he's doing a good job by society's standards. He's playing his role well. The fact that the role causes damage is of relatively little importance.

Feminist Dale Spender has said before that when the experiences of women or queer people go unnamed, people doubt their existence at all. Before we had labels like "sexism," "sexual harassment," and "homophobia"— terms that have only existed since the 1960s and '70s—people saw the victims' behavior as the problem. Women were hypersensitive and neurotic (or "asking for it") and gay people were abominable. But even after we give these experiences names and recognition, we often still treat them as the victim's responsibility to fix. We teach women that if you feel silenced at work, or in your relationship, or just walking from the train to your apartment, then it's your job, and your job alone, to find a way to be heard. Do as Elizabeth Warren did in 2017 when Mitch McConnell silenced her on the Senate floor, and *nevertheless persist*. Speak out on social media, start your own organizations, take to the streets. Tell the sexual trespassers, "No."

I'd like to take a moment to offer a brief linguistic critique of what's wrong with teaching women to say "no" and men to listen for "no" when we talk about sexual consent: analyses of real-life refusals show that there is a precise formula English speakers follow to decline things in a socially acceptable way, and it actually almost never includes the word *no*. Instead, it goes: hesitate + hedge + express regret + give a culturally acceptable reason. As in "Um, well, I'd love to, but I have to finish this assignment," or "Oh, I'm sorry, but I should go home and feed my cat." It is also our very job as listeners to make inferences about what other people mean when they speak, whether or not it is said in the clearest way. (Think of how strange it would be to reject a friend's invitation out to coffee with a blunt "NO!") Not to mention that in a sexual assault scenario, refusing something so brusquely might cause more tension or danger. The problem with teaching "no means no" is that it ultimately lets sexual offenders off the hook, because it removes their duty to use common sense as listeners, so that later they can say, "Well, she didn't say 'no.' I can't read people's minds," and we as a culture go, "That's true, her fault." Plus, as we've already learned, sexual trespassers actually don't need an explicit *no*—they already get what they're doing is wrong. They simply don't care, because our culture teaches them that they don't have to.

Inspiring marginalized folks to self-advocate loudly and clearly is important, of course. It is indispensable. But in practice, it only solves the problem halfway. Because what it fails to address is that we live in a culture that doesn't exactly make it easy for women and queer folks to stand up for themselves in the first place.

Peg O'Connor, a gender and philosophy scholar at Gustavus Adolphus College in Minnesota, explains it like this: "We are not all Elizabeth Warren either in temperament or situation. Too many women would be fired from their jobs were they to speak out. In their personal relationships, women often fear the consequences of speaking out too." The fear of being punished for speaking against the status quo is all-encompassing, and ultimately it works to control women's actions from the inside out. It makes women silence themselves. "This is in no sense blaming the victim," O'Connor explains, "but rather an acknowledgment of the way that dominated or oppressed people often 'self-police' or become 'docile.'"

What's more is that thanks to centuries of steeping in messages that women are delicate, overly emotional, and unfit to hold power, many women have an internalized belief that it's natural for them not to have a voice. It's an unconscious feeling that speechlessness is just part of being a woman and that to be too loud or assertive would mean losing female identity, which is precious, because it's a huge part of who they are.

In a perfect world, people wouldn't need to strategize

what ghoulish faces or clever interview questions to have on hand for whenever a stranger in the street ambushes them with a review of how their butt looks in their jeans. In such a world, sex and flirting would be things that were equally desired and agreed upon, and preaching the necessity of "yes/no" consent transactions would no longer apply because it would already be a given that each sexual participant took the time and empathy to get on each other's wavelength. The word *hysterical* would retire alongside *old maid* and *spinster* to the graveyard of forgotten offenses, and everyone, regardless of gender, would feel like they had access to the mic whenever they had something important to say.

The way to get to that world starts not with teaching women how to protect themselves from harm but with teaching men, ideally from very early on, that the whole world does not belong to them. When men are itty-bitty boys, we as their parents and teachers have to dismantle our culture's ideas of masculinity as we know them at every turn. It has to be okay— encouraged, really—for men to empathize and align with women and to stick up for them when they see other men try to take them down, linguistically and otherwise. "To put their principles above their fraternal loyalties," as Deborah Cameron once put it. And it has to be *not* okay to treat anyone who isn't a man like an intruder in their world.

In 2015 Sheryl Sandberg told a story to the *New York Times* about a guy named Glen Mazzara, who ran a hit TV series called *The Shield*. Mazzara noticed that in pitch meetings, the show's two women writers never spoke up. So he pulled them aside and encouraged them not to be so shy. It wasn't a matter of "shy," they promised. As Mazzara soon observed, nearly every time one of the women tried to pitch something, she was either interrupted, shot down, or her idea was stolen and taken credit for by one of the guys before she could finish. Mazzara was a busy fellow, and he could have ignored these women, or told them just to practice getting better at asserting themselves; but instead, he tried to help by switching up the power dynamics of the room so that they could be heard. He established a no-interruption rule in the writer's room, so that no one was allowed to cut off anyone of any gender before they were done speaking. As it turned out, the new strategy worked, the women's ideas became heard, and it made the whole team more productive and creative.

Men in power should see it as their responsibility to extend a hand in this way, because in the end, they too might have something to gain from mixing up the voices in the room. Take a cue from one of the most powerful men in US history: at the end of a 2014 press conference, President Barack Obama called on eight reporters for questions—all women. The act made international headlines. "Had a politician given only men a chance to ask questions, it would not have been news; it would have been a regular day," Sheryl Sandberg commented. "We wonder what would happen if we all held Obama-style meetings, offering women the floor whenever possible."

That's not to say that while men sort this whole thing out, women should all go on a big Carnival Cruise and bide their time slurping piña coladas out of sippy cups shaped like vaginas until the matrilineal revolution takes hold. Don't get me wrong, that sounds like a blast. But realistically, we have to stick up for ourselves along the way too. We have to speak out when wronged, believe one another, apply for positions of power, and hire each other. Robin Lakoff wrote in 1992: "As long as we are complicit in our own voicelessness, there is no incentive, neither fear nor shame, to make anyone else change."

The process of gaining a voice that people will listen to and respect isn't simple, but that doesn't mean it has to be a drag. Language is fun, after all, and—other than shouting "fire" in a movie theater—there are very few laws controlling what words we're allowed to say. This is especially good news for those who get a kick out of speaking in ways that not everyone finds so "appropriate," which, in my opinion, is sometimes the single most feminist thing you can do with language.

Get ready for some delicious inappropriateness: if the

Motion Picture Association of America were to assign a rating to the following chapter (which I'm terribly glad they didn't—good thing books don't receive ratings like movies do, right?), you can be sure it would be a solid R for vulgarity.

fuck it

an ode to cursing while female

> A whistling sailor, a crowing hen, and a
> swearing woman ought all three to go to
> hell together.
>
> —*American proverb*

Dr. Richard Stephens and his research team have proven me right once and for all. They published a 2017 paper in the *Personality and Individual Differences* journal about the relationship between personality type and common everyday habits. Based on a survey of a thousand participants, Stephens's study draws a variety of correlations between different human traits and behaviors, like an affinity for dirty jokes to extroversion and a tendency to sing in the shower to agreeability. But the best correlation of them all, to me at least, is this: people with high IQs, the most intelligent folks of the bunch, are more likely than anyone else to curse.

This correlation feels personal. Like most American children, I grew up with the narrative, promoted by high school teachers and friends' hard-ass dads, that a high incidence of cursing meant you were angry, crass, unladylike, and had a limited vocabulary. I certainly wanted people to think of me as smart and elegant, but I was also suspicious of this claim. Admittedly, I have one of the foulest mouths of anyone I know. When I was nine, a girl at recess dared me to say *shit* to a lunch lady—I did; I didn't get in trouble—and I've been hooked on four-letter words ever since. To me, Stephens's findings were excellent news. I even shared them on Facebook, secretly hoping that my twelfth-grade English teacher would click.

The majority of English curse words fall into three main semantic categories, which reflect the particular anxieties and fascinations of our culture. These categories include sex (*fuck*, *dick*, *cunt*), scatology (*shit*, *crap*, *asshole*), and religion (*goddamnit*, *holy shit*, *Christ on a cracker*).* I was made well aware throughout my

---

* My favorite example of religious-themed curse words comes from French-speaking Canada. Their strongest swears are based on traditional Catholic props, including *tabarnak*, meaning "tabernacle," and *j'men calice*, meaning "I don't give a chalice."

youthhood that hearing such things come out of a little girl's mouth was inappropriate, impolite, and—most frustratingly—adorable. Still, nothing in the world could squash my zest for profanity. As a kid, I remember eavesdropping on my parents' rated R movies or catching an adult at the grocery store drop a jar of pickles—"Shit!"—and quietly practicing these words to myself. The opening bursts and closing thwacks bookending terms like *bitch*, *fuck*, and *dick* felt like a party in the mouth (the word *fuck* alone makes use of the lips, the tongue, *and* the teeth). It was linguistic calisthenics. And it was "grown-up language"—off-limits for kids. Nothing could have made it more appealing.

Years later, in college, I learned about the concept of *phonosymbolism*, which says that certain speech sounds can hold meaning in and of themselves. Think of the inherent harshness conveyed by a word like *chop* or *slap*, the ooey-gooeyness of *slither*, and the coziness in *velvet*. Swears had this snap, crackle, pop that absolutely tickled me—not to mention their grammatical versatility. *Fuck*, for example, is not only fun to say all on its own, it's also one of the most malleable words in the English language, able to slot naturally into almost any grammatical category to communicate the desired sentiment. You can use it as a noun ("You crazy fuck!"), a verb ("This traffic is totally fucking me"), an adverb ("I fucking nailed that!"), an adjective ("This situation is totally fucked up"), or an interjection ("*Fuuuuuuuck*"). If you're as habitual a *fuck* user as I am, you might even

wordslut

use it as a discourse marker or filler word, like *um* or *well*. As in, "Fuck, so, you want to get some pizza later?"

Contrary to what teachers and parents might proselytize, I'm willing to bet that English speakers who can curse fluently have a more creative grasp of the language as a whole. Here's one of my favorite cursing facts from Phonology 101: swears are the only types of English words that you can use as an *infix*. An infix is a grammatical unit of meaning that you insert in the middle of a word, similar to a prefix, which comes at the beginning (like the "un" in "unusual"), or a suffix, which comes at the end (like the "ful" in "grateful"). There are plenty of foreign languages that use infixes all over the place, but in English, we only have two: *fucking* and *damn*. An example: "I'll guaran-damn-tee you that you're gonna love Cali-fucking-fornia."

Cursing is a word nerd's dream, and yet . . . so controversial. To me, our culture's horror surrounding taboo language—the alarmist bleeping on network TV, the image of mothers washing their kids' mouths out with soap—has generally seemed a little . . . *puritanical*. Blown out of proportion. After all, there is a big difference between a swear word and an insult. There is overlap, but as we learned in chapter 1, just as you can insult someone without cursing (*nasty, wimp, pansy*), you can curse without insulting.

Linguistic studies show that in modern practice, it's actually quite rare for swearing to intend hostility or offense; instead, cursing is an incredibly complex, colorful language category that can serve nearly infinite emotional purposes—humor, shock, sadness, solidarity—some of which might be considered actively polite, depending on the context. Oftentimes, curse words are used to foster social harmony, like if you were to tell someone, "That is a fucking brilliant idea," or "These cupcakes are the shit." Linguists say the only impolite sorts of cursing come when you purposefully threaten someone ("Don't fucking talk to me like that," "Back off, bitch"), express strong emotions in public, or have misunderstood the social rules of a certain situation. As a whole, though, the majority of everyday cursing instances in the twenty-first century are not considered inappropriate. As a pair of researchers named Timothy Jay and Kristin Janschewitz wrote in 2008, "Through thousands of incidents of recorded swearing, we have never witnessed any form of physical aggression as a consequence of [it]."

Historically, however, attitudes toward cursing—particularly when women do it—have not always been so positive. Since swearing is largely thought to be intrinsically aggressive, women who do it may be perceived as breaking the traditional rules of femininity, which require them to be sweet, deferential, and constantly attuned to the feelings of others. Naturally, defying this expectation can invite criticism. I, for one, have been told several times that I "curse like a man," and I can never tell whether this is a compliment or not.

The idea that swearing is inherently masculine has a long history. While one can presume that language taboos have always existed, vulgarity wasn't fully born until the Middle Ages, when courtly traditions created gentility and thus a new value for "clean" speech. The same standards for refinement that strengthened linguistic taboos also put women on a proverbial pedestal, meaning that their use of potty words, and men's use of potty words in their presence, became a major no-no.

Even Shakespeare poked fun at the cultural cliché that women's mouths and ears were too delicate for cursing. In *Henry IV*, the character Hotspur teases his wife, Lady Percy, for her low-class use of oaths: "Come, Kate, I'll have your song too," he says. "Not mine, in good sooth," she replies, to which Hotspur says, "Not yours, in good sooth! Heart! You swear like a comfit-maker's wife! . . . Swear me, Kate, like a lady as thou art, a good mouth-filling oath."

By having Hotspur beseech Lady Percy not to swear like a lowly comfit-maker's wife, but instead like an aristocratic "lady," Shakespeare demonstrated an awareness that people connect swearing not only to gender, but also to social class. The popular opinion was that poorer folks cursed more often than and in a different manner from the wealthy. Centuries later, English speakers still hold this presumption. A 1997 study of gender and cursing revealed that listeners associated sailor-mouthed women not only with lower socioeconomic status but also with lower moral standing. The implication was that a woman partial to dropping the *f*-bomb would be more likely to, say, litter or cheat on her spouse than one who wasn't. (This result was not found in participants' judgments of men who cursed.)

Even a few linguists have believed there to be inherent "women's" and "men's" styles of vulgarity (and that those who disobeyed these rules were violating their very nature). Our old buddy Otto Jespersen wrote in 1922 that women have an "instinctive shrinking from coarse and gross expressions and [a] preference for refined and (in certain spheres) veiled and indirect expressions." Robin Lakoff gave a similar take in *Language and Woman's Place*, where she noted that, because women have for so long been socialized to speak more politely, they are more likely to say things like "good grief" and "oh, shucks," while men say "goddamnit" and "holy shit." To Lakoff, women's watered-down curses were less powerful, less communicative, and thus more ladylike—and they reflected their position in society as weaklings and whiners. "Women don't use off-color or indelicate expressions," she stated.

These misconceptions about women and vulgarity might seem fairly inconsequential, but they can have serious real-life repercussions. A 1991 study of sexual harassment in an underground coal mine determined that one of the biggest obstacles to women miners' professional advancement was that their male colleagues ousted them from social interaction on the basis that they were too sensitive to swear. Paradoxically, the study also found that if these women started swearing, it didn't earn them the same social status as their male colleagues; instead, it actually heightened their femininity by way of juxtaposition. In other words, by adopting this one "masculine" trait (vulgarity), their visibility as women increased in comparison, like Charlie's Angels with their long hair, skintight outfits, and nine-millimeter pistols. Ever met a guy who thought a feminine-presenting woman who could shoot a gun or smoke a cigar was hot? Same idea: the study found that male coal miners actually interpreted the female miners' swearing as an invitation, and women who cursed were sexually harassed significantly more than women who didn't. Those who opted out of swearing entirely didn't have it much better, though; they were excluded from conversation, participation, and ultimately power. As one female miner told the researchers, "Filthy language is like an invisible line between men and women." The women miners ultimately found themselves between a rock and a hard place—to swear or not to swear. Either way, they couldn't win.

In normal everyday life, gendered differences in cursing usage aren't as extreme as they were in that coal mine environment. Linguists have discovered that *context*, rather than gender, is the biggest factor in determining how most people really swear. It's one of the first lessons in vulgarity that kids learn when they figure out they can swear more liberally at recess than in math class. What Jespersen, Lakoff, and plenty of other modern listeners have failed to realize is that women are game to have just as much R-rated fun with language as men—there's nothing about the fundamentals of female-ness that cause a person to say *fiddlesticks* instead of *fuck*. Studies of modern cursing consistently show that everyone who swears does it with equal strength. The one and only disparity is that the motivation underlying women's use of these words is slightly—but meaningfully—different.

Why people curse is a topic taken up by Karyn Stapleton, a social psychology scholar at Ulster University in Ireland. In 2003, Stapleton conducted a survey of swearing practices by men and women in an urban Irish town, interviewing a group of thirty men and thirty women on their swearing habits. For the crowd she was studying, swearing was a common daily practice—most individual swear words were not considered obscene, and men and women participated in cursing equally.

But what motivated each gender's swearing was a different story. Stapleton sat each of her subjects down and asked them to self-report why they curse in the first place. She collected their responses, organized them by theme, and placed them in a chart, which I've included on the next page.

Here are the points I find most intriguing: first, while about half of Stapleton's male respondents reported that they swore out of habit or because it was simply expected, very few women reported the same. Instead, Stapleton's female subjects described swearing as a part of their individual personalities (and if someone asked me why I swore, I would say the same thing). In

wordslut

SHIT, DO I
SWEAR TOO
MUCH?

FUCK NO!

MEN'S AND WOMEN'S SELF-REPORTED
REASONS FOR CURSING

REASONS	NO. OF WOMEN	NO. OF MEN	TOTAL	EXAMPLES
HUMOR/STORY TELLING	15	13	28	"WHEN YOU'RE TELLING A GOOD STORY AND YOU WANT TO GET A LAUGH."
TO CREATE EMPHASIS	13	11	24	"IT HELPS TO GET YOUR MESSAGE ACROSS."
ANGER/TENSION RELEASE	10	10	20	"IT'S LIKE WHEN YOU'RE REALLY PISSED OFF—A SORT OF RELEASE."
HABIT	4	14	18	"IT'S JUST SOMETHING I DO—I'M NOT EVEN AWARE OF IT ANYMORE."
IT'S NORMAL/EXPECTED	2	16	18	"EVERYBODY CURSES THESE DAYS— IT WOULD BE MORE UNUSUAL IF YOU DIDN'T."
TO SHOW INTIMACY/TRUST	12	0	12	"I THINK IT SHOWS THAT YOU HAVE A FAIRLY CLOSE RELATIONSHIP."
TO COVER FEAR/VULNERABILITY	6	5	11	"IT'S LIKE A DEFENSE—TO COVER UP HOW YOU REALLY FEEL."
PART OF PERSONALITY	6	0	6	"IT'S JUST SOMETHING PEOPLE KNOW ME BY."
TO SHOCK	2	1	3	"IT'S REALLY EFFECTIVE IF THE OTHER PERSON DOESN'T SWEAR AT ALL—IT'S THE SHOCK FACTOR, I SUPPOSE."

a subtle but important way, this is different from the men's view that swearing is "normal and expected," because it shows women's awareness that swearing will likely be seen as a sort of unique, perhaps deviant quirk and not something natural or predictable, like it is for men. Thus, for women, swearing plays a part in constructing a particular type of identity.

Another of the top reasons women gave for cursing, one that wasn't reported by a single man, was to show intimacy and trust. Women are aware that in a lot of situations they could get in trouble, or at least a sideways look, for swearing. They are "contextually constrained to a greater extent than men," Stapleton said. For women, it takes a special group, often in a private space, to be able to swear freely without judgment; thus a certain amount of trust is required for them to let down their filter. In some situations, cursing may serve as an act of solidarity or even affection between women friends, which isn't usually the case for dudes.

Stapleton also asked her subjects why they might *avoid* certain curse words—specifically the more "obscene" ones, which participants agreed were the words that made reference to the vagina (*cunt, fanny**). The top three reasons women gave were that they found these terms sexist because they gave a negative impression, and because they made them feel uncomfortable. For men, the top reasons were that they found them inappropriate in certain company, that they were sexist, and finally that they made them *appear* sexist. This last reason is particularly interesting, because there was not a single woman in the study who gave that as a response. For twice the number of women as men, sexism itself, as opposed to the motivation not to *seem* sexist, was reason enough to avoid certain swears.

---

* Indeed, across the pond, what America would consider a squeaky-clean word for your backside is actually a semi-lewd term for the frontside.

wordslut

In a big way, women's avoidance of sexist swear words is another symbol of unity and mutual support among women. As Stapleton analyzed, "A discourse of female solidarity is evident here in that women who use offensive expletives are looked upon [by other women] with more disdain than men." According to this study, women don't want to betray the tribe by using words like *cunt* so liberally, and they seem disappointed in other women who do. As one twenty-six-year-old participant named Kelly said, "Women may be seen as 'letting the side down' if they engage in the use of certain terms." It would be a sign that they hadn't really thought about what the word meant. Women don't expect men to know better or try to understand the potential harm of what they're saying, but they do expect this of other women.

A reasonable takeaway from Stapleton's study: women rarely curse for no reason. The *shits* and *motherfucks* aren't there just because they're "expected" or to use obscenity for obscenity's sake. They're there to make someone laugh, to put on a brave face, to feel close to someone, to be an individual. For women, choosing which swear words to embrace and which to reject is part of an ongoing negotiation of femininity itself. As Stapleton wrote, "In addition to contesting social norms of femininity, the use of 'bad language' may also function to construct and en-act new modes and versions of 'being a woman.'"

The observations Laurel A. Sutton made in the 1990s of how women used *bitch* and *ho* with their friends showed that women's cursing wasn't just a case of women regurgitating how men use these terms. Instead, women were imitating other women whom they admired, women who challenged the stereotypical image of a well-mannered "lady," like Trina and Rihanna and the badass women in their communities. Swearing works as a way for women to figure out what kind of women they are. To define their femininity on their own terms.

And yet, as fun and useful as swear words can be, we can't ignore that the ones currently offered by the English language aren't exactly perfect. As much as I personally love to curse and consider it a part of who I am—as much as I delight in snarkily telling people "fuck you" and "suck my dick"—I can't help but notice that most of our lexicon's most powerful curse words weren't exactly invented with me as the speaker in mind. Phrases like "suck my dick" and "fuck your mother" are part of the largest category of English curse words, the sexual category, which as it stands only represents one point of view.

Many of our language's most potent phrases—from *pussy* to *motherfucker*—paint a picture of women, men, and sex from a cisgender dude's perspective. They portray the act of sex as inherently penetrative, the penis as violent and powerful, and the vagina as weak and passive. The word *pussy* doesn't portray the complexity of the vulva, or the parts of it generally considered most important to those who actually have vulvas (clits, G-spots). Instead, it's just a vague, kitty-cat-like place for a penis to go. Meanwhile, phrases like "fuck you in the ass" or "suck it, bitch," both of which imply an erect phallus, create the impression that language is only powerful when male sex organs are involved. It would be extremely unique to hear someone say "eat my pussy" or "drown in my G-spot" to achieve the same effect as these phallic expressions. One could certainly get away with saying "suck my dick" for humor or emphasis without it seeming sexual, but the same could not be said for "eat my pussy"—evidence that there is a semantic imbalance between curse words from a normatively male perspective and curse words from a normatively female one.

In a 1999 essay on feminist vulgarity, activist Erika Fricke said that swearing as we know it mirrors our culture's clichés about gender, bodies, and sex in general. "Whether the stereotype is that women don't like sex and men always have to wheedle it out of them; that women 'get attached,' while to men sex is meaningless; or that women's internal genitalia and potential to be pregnant makes them more introspective and nurturing, while men are brash and achievement focused . . . vulgarity becomes a microcosm of all these questions of divided genders in conflict," she wrote. Ultimately, most contemporary cursing simply does not succeed in reflecting the bodies, sexual participation, or fantasies of anyone who isn't a man with a boner. And thus, the power of vulgarity ends up working mostly in service of dudes.

In pursuit of a more feminist swear vocabulary, we have a few options, the least exciting of which is probably just to limit one's cursing to the scatology category. The *shits*, *pisses*, *assholes*, and other bodily function metaphors are all perfectly gender neutral. In my opinion, though, the sexual ones are simply . . . more fun.

There have been quite a few women throughout history who've attempted to co-opt our existing curse words to reflect their own sexuality. In the 1990s Madonna would scream profanities and simulate masturbation onstage to the admiration of both feminists and teenage boys. ("*Fuck* is not a bad word!" she declaimed before thousands of fans on her 1990 Blond Ambition tour. "*Fuck* is a *good* word! *Fuck* is why I am here. *Fuck* is why YOU are here! . . . So get over it, o-fucking-kay?!") However, Fricke points out that for women, power derived from sexuality can be a double-edged sword. You can't explain to a fourteen-year-old boy that Madonna's sexual expression is a feminist thing (at least not in the moment); to him, it will just seem sexy. Boldly expressing your sexuality as a woman is most certainly not a problem, but, frustratingly, it doesn't read as quite the same breed of power exerted when men say "suck my cock."

So here's my favorite strategy: people who don't feel as though our current curse words consider or empower their bodies can invent a brand-new set of terms that do. The word *clit*, for one, has all the makings of a lovable curse word—it's monosyllabic and plosive, just like *dick* and *fuck*. By shouting "suck my clit," instead of "suck my dick," women (or anyone with a clit) can flip around the POV in a phonetically satisfying manner. As Fricke points out, "'Clit' sounds like the kind of body part that would take action and, combined with colorful phrasing and the right tone of voice, could come off as pretty damn degrading."* Or fun, punchy, and full of humor if that's the intent. Maybe from now on we should all say "holy clit."

On that note, if you want to make things really interesting, you could even hybridize both feminine and masculine metaphors to come up with some cool Frankensteinian compound swear. *Clitfuck* has a certain ring to it. Or maybe *dicksnatch*? I could play this game for hours.

This isn't a call for everyone to rewrite the rules of cursing overnight. Everyone's relationships to individual swears are varied and complex, and just as it is perfectly reasonable to find words like *cunt* and *motherfucker* offensive, or to want to move away from vulgar phrases that imply violence or homophobia ("fuck you in the ass," etc.), it's also permissible to actively enjoy and not resent the idea that hardcore cursing is not necessarily expected of women. For some, the fact that women can use cursing to craft their personalities or to highlight their femininity will seem problematic; to others, it will

---

* I tend to curse more out of joy than anger, but if you want to go the aggressive route with your feminist swears, Fricke suggests that women "victimize" the male organ—"For example, 'Shove a catheter up it.'" For this strategy to work, she says it should always be called a *penis* or something that sounds equally soft, limp, and devoid of the strong stop consonants in *dick* and *cock*.

feel empowering. We can think of these reinventions of mainstream curse words and studies on gendered swearing practices not as a call to blanket abolish our existing glossary of vulgarities but rather as an invitation to think consciously about the messages we wish to put out in the world when R-rated utterances leave our mouths. Think of it as a fun challenge to swear with intention, to further prove Dr. Richard Stephens right with the notion that the smartest English speakers are also the crassest—especially those who curse like feminists.

No matter what, there is a 97 to 99 percent chance that I am going to incorporate the phrase "holy clit" into my vocabulary. And if that's a move toward progress, my lifelong potty mouth and I are glad to be involved.

"cackling" clinton and "sexy" scarjo

the struggle of being a woman in public

On an unseasonably warm fall day in 2015, *BroBible*, a blog for millennial men whose breed of content is exactly what it sounds like (fratty, dogmatic), publishes an article ranking the ten sexiest female voices in Hollywood. These women are "like candy for your ears," the headline promises. The brief post introduces a YouTube video counting down movie stars whose voices increasingly "drive the men wild with their seductiveness." "We could listen to these ladies talk allll day long," the *BroBible* author writes. "From Catherine Zeta-Jones to Penélope Cruz to the always lovable Emma Stone, these women have voices that stir up something special when we hear them speak."

The video's narrator decrees that the qualities making a woman's voice a *BroBible*-worthy turn-on include foreign accents (particularly British ones), low whispery cadences, and raspiness. The featured actresses' voices are soft, relaxed, and a little hoarse, as if they might be overcoming a bout of laryngitis, or have just finished a lengthy session of moaning and are all tuckered out, rendering them unable to speak any louder than a gentle bedside murmur.

I, too, think women with raspy voices hit the audio lottery, but I have to wonder why: blind tests have consistently shown that higher-pitched voices are preferable in women (a sign of youth and small physical size; better for breeding). Then again, more recent studies have found that in romantic social interactions (I think they call that flirting?), women actively lower their pitch. A series of 2014 experiments out of Pennsylvania revealed that across the board, English speakers associate deep, raspy voices with seduction. (Amusingly, they also found that only women have the ability to put on a "sexy" vocal affect; apparently, listeners think it just sounds silly when men do it.) Researchers weren't able to pinpoint exactly why we've all come to the conclusion that a raspy voice on a woman is so hot. I have a personal theory that it's because it sounds like your morning voice, the voice you wake up with after sleeping next to someone (and maybe doing other stuff). It's a sign of intimacy. People hear that voice and they picture you in bed.

I was listening to these clips of Charlize Theron and Stones (both Sharon and Emma) through headphones on the couch next to my best friend, and after the video finished, I leaned over and asked her to name which Hollywood actress she thinks has the sexiest voice. "Scarlett Johansson," she said. Indeed, Ms. Johansson, who lent her husky tenor, the sweetest of all ear candy, to the voice-only role of Samantha in 2013's *Her*, earned the number one spot on *BroBible*'s list.

A little less than a year after ScarJo's voice is christened Hollywood's hottest, the owner of the *unsexiest* female voice in modern history is also chosen: Hillary Clinton. (*BroBible* isn't involved in the decision this time, but politics isn't really their beat.) The verdict is made official on July 28, 2016, the same evening that Clinton accepts her victory as the first-ever female presidential nominee. "It is with humility, determination, and boundless confidence in America's promise that I accept your nomination for president of the United States," she proclaims.

To me, the fervor in Clinton's voice matches the gravity of the occasion, but for several garrulous male pundits, it symbolizes a different honor—that of America's least fuckable-sounding lady. Many of the tweets and comments that follow Clinton's speech describe not its content but its delivery, categorizing her voice as "shrill," "shouting," and "not so attractive." Journalist Steve Clemons instructs Clinton to "modulate" her tone. MSNBC host Joe Scarborough suggests that she "smile." Trump calls her speech a "very average scream."

By late 2016, so much had been said about the unlikability of Hillary Clinton's voice that the subject had become as much a cultural-wide meme as Kylie Jenner's lips or JLo's derriere. Or, as it were, Scarlett Johansson's voice for the opposite reason. These two women's voices actually represent a real conundrum that exists for women in the public eye: women who wish to hold power are expected to strike a precarious balance of appearing pleasant and polite, like the sweet-tempered caregivers they're used to women being, as well as tough and authoritative, like capable leaders, all the while doing their best to convince everyone that they're neither a bitch (Hillary Clinton) nor a sexual object (Scarlett Johansson). "The two things clash, and women can be negatively judged for erring too far in either direction," comments our Oxford linguist Deborah Cameron. "It's a very difficult line to walk."

This tricky negotiation of traditional femininity, which has historically been backdropped by a private setting, and confident leadership, which is a public enterprise, is one that social scientists have termed the "double bind."

Most women who pursue a high-profile career end up falling on one side of the double bind or the other. While Clinton is perhaps the best-known modern public figure to have endured her level of linguistic criticism, she is certainly not the first. Other women who've shed tradi-tionally feminine vocal traits to be seen as tough leaders but were in turn pegged as cold and overbearing include Elizabeth I (The Virgin Queen), Margaret Thatcher (The Iron Lady), Supreme Court Justice Sonia Sotomayor, British Prime Minister Theresa May (dubbed by Twitter as an "evil witch queen"), and politician Janet Napoli-tano, whom journalist Andrew Napolitano (no relation) nicknamed "Evil Cousin Janet." No one ever questioned these women's strength, but it came at the expense of their likability.

On the other end of the double bind, when a woman in charge makes no attempt to conduct herself in a "mas-culine" fashion, or perhaps even highlights her femi-ninity, she will be perceived as fragile and out of her depth. But, because she is hanging on to most of her normatively ladylike traits, she will also seem less scary. As her perceived toughness dips, her likability spikes.

No matter a woman's delivery, cultures through the ages and the world share a tradition of informing female politicians, news anchors, business leaders, and other women who venture to speak in public that they need to please pipe down. In the early twentieth century, a sur-vey of talk radio listeners reported that 100 out of 101 respondents preferred male hosts' voices over women's, lamenting that the women's voices were "shrill" (just like Clinton's ninety years later) and that their voices demonstrated "too much" personality. A 2016 report from *Time* magazine found that in ancient Greece, female

"cackling" clinton and "sexy" scarjo

outspokenness was associated with "prostitution, madness, witchcraft, and androgyny." During the Middle Ages, there was a special English word for women who dared to speak in public: they were labeled *scolds*, meaning women unable to keep their "negative" or "insubordinate" words to themselves.

In 2016 linguist Nic Subtirelu took an empirical gander at the current media's use of the words *shrill*, *shriek*, and *screech* to describe public figures' voices and found that commentators are 2.17 to 3.14 times likelier to characterize a woman using this language than a man. These words, as well as *bossy*, *grating*, *caterwauling*, and *abrasive*, technically may target the volume or timbre of one's voice, but linguists know the criticism goes deeper than that. Biases against the voices of powerful women are, again, actually related not to the quality of the voice itself but instead to our impressions of gender and authority at large. "For historical and social reasons, the 'unmarked' or default voice of authority is a male voice," says Cameron. "Criticism of female politicians' voices is essentially a way of tapping into the still widely held belief that women do not have the authority to lead."

Admittedly, even I find myself responding more positively, with more reverence I suppose, whenever I hear a deep male voice (it's half the reason I tune into Roman Mars's richly narrated architecture podcast, *99% Invisible*. And don't even get me started on the iconic audio stylings of Morgan Freeman). Researchers have determined that one of the reasons we tend to connect men's voices with authority is that we connect low pitch with authority.

Pitch is unique as a vocal quality, because unlike volume, tone, or even a person's native language, it is perhaps the only thing about one's speech that is determined (or at least influenced) by physiology. On average, men's vocal folds tend to be a few millimeters longer than women's. Linguists have found that low pitch is something we associate with larger physical size* (compare the bark of a German shepherd with that of a Chihuahua) as well as dominance and capability (picture news anchor Walter Cronkite). A 2012 study using digitally altered recordings of men's and women's voices saying, "I urge you to vote for me this November," revealed that listeners preferred the deeper versions—evidence that we're more likely to blindly heed the urgings of a low-pitched statement, regardless of who might be saying it. It is for this reason that men—or anyone, for that matter—often actively lower their pitch (sometimes consciously, sometimes not) when they wish to appear more authoritative.

High pitch, by contrast, is a key marker of smaller size (again, the Chihuahua), immaturity (like the voice of a child), and excessive emotion (squeals of joy, excitement, fear). As Cameron says, "Saying that a woman's voice is 'shrill' is also a code for 'she's not in control.'"

---

* Studies show that taller folks often have bigger, lower airways and lungs, and that extra space produces a deeper sound. Bigger men don't *always* have lower-pitched voices, though. Have you ever analyzed the speech of British soccer player David Beckham? Very manly guy, surprisingly dainty voice.

This is ultimately why Britain's first woman prime minister, Margaret Thatcher, took vocal lessons to learn how to lower her pitch while speaking in public. She hoped this would earn her the sort of respect that the digitally manipulated recordings of women's voices in 2012 did. To say the least, not everybody was so fond of the result. But Thatcher's pitch, like Clinton's "shrillness," was not really the main issue: that she was a woman in charge in the first place was significantly more of a problem.

Criticisms of women's voices don't end when the speakers sound more traditionally feminine either. A 1995 *New York Times* story told of a group of elevator operators at a department store in Japan who, as a part of their job, trained to raise their pitch in order to sound "cuter," more "girlish," and more "polite." The *Times* described, "European women no longer rearrange their bodies with corsets, and Chinese no longer cripple their daughters by binding their feet. But many Japanese women speak well above their natural pitch, especially in formal settings, on the phone, or when dealing with customers." Despite all the effort, when asked about the elevator operators' honeyed falsetto, a Tokyo interpreter responded, "Those girls are trained to be robots. With the elevator girls, you don't see a person but a doll."

Doll metaphors are a go-to for critics of women who fall on the more classically feminine side of the double bind. In 2016 journalist Ben Shapiro wrote an article titled "Yes, Hillary Clinton is shrill. No, it's not sexist to say so" with the rationale that calling Clinton shrill is kosher because it's simply "reality," as proven by the fact that this word is not used to describe every woman in politics. "Nobody calls Senator Dianne Feinstein (D-CA) shrill, because she's not shrill," Shapiro defended. "She may have lifeless eyes, a doll's eyes, but she doesn't shriek like a wounded seagull." *Lifeless doll eyes.* But right, no, not sexist at all.

Probably the clearest illustration of the two sides of the linguistic double bind presented itself in 2008, when Hillary Clinton campaigned for president at the same time as Governor Sarah Palin, John McCain's running mate. The juxtaposition of these two women was so extreme it was as if a gender studies professor had dreamed it up specifically for argument's sake. As 1984's winner of Miss Wasilla and Miss Congeniality, beauty queen Palin was a tailor-made foil to Clinton, whose very laughter, according to several male commentators, made "her sound like the Wicked Witch of the West." The "Clinton cackle" was a phrase commonly used every time she so much as cracked a smile. (And over the years, similar witch comparisons have been made to Theresa May, Kellyanne Conway, and Senator Elizabeth Warren, who was once the subject of a terrific fake news story claiming that she regularly participated in nude pagan rituals as a college student.)

As political scientist Elvin T. Lim wrote in 2009, "There may be objective reasons for thinking Clinton to be unlikable and competent and Palin to be likable

but incompetent, but it is surely more than a coincidence that the two most prominent women in American politics in 2008 so perfectly occupied the two sides of the double bind."

If you've ever had a woman boss (especially one in her twenties or thirties who's new to being in charge), you've likely witnessed her struggle to negotiate the double bind firsthand. I've often noticed it in how younger female higher-ups word their emails. An example: let's say a manager wanted to assign a project with a tight deadline to her assistant. She could phrase her email with a straightforward tone and no-frills punctuation—"The project needs to be done by tomorrow at 3 p.m. Thanks."—but, because we have certain expectations of how women are supposed to communicate (politely, indirectly), that might earn her a reputation as a cold bitch. On the other hand, she could pepper her email with hedges, exclamation points, and emoji— "If you could possibly have the project finished by to-morrow at 3 p.m., that'd be AMAZING. Thank you so much!!)"—but, because we have certain expectations of how bosses are supposed to communicate (bluntly, directly), that might make her seem jumpy and unfit to lead. Of course, there are plenty of male bosses who grapple with how to conduct themselves linguistically in the workplace, but, because our visions of masculine speech and authoritative speech align better, this negotiation isn't usually as tricky for them.

Our conflicted attitudes toward powerful women sprout from many sources. Obviously, there is no one simple explanation, but Deborah Cameron suggests that our resistance to women in positions of authority, and the reason the double bind itself exists, is in part related to the messy clash of feelings we have about our own mothers. "Our main historical model for female authority is the maternal variety," she explains, "and it's a form of power most people are at least somewhat ambivalent about, because we've all experienced the powerlessness of the child and the rebellion against maternal power which is part of growing up."

The negative language we use to describe "domineering" women—*shrew, bitch, witch, cunt*—sounds not unlike the words we might have used (or at least thought about using) when our moms took away our car privileges or made us do our homework. When adults wield these words to describe female politicians, they're implying how crazy and wrong it is when women assert their authority outside the home, just as terms like *pussywhipped* and *henpecked* imply how crazy and wrong it is when men allow them to do so.

I don't mean to imply that the voices of powerful

women are the only ones that get critiqued—men get some flack too. Over the years, linguists and commentators have dedicated plenty of effort to analyzing Trump's speech. A 2016 *Slate* piece called "Trump's Tower of Babble" cited an analysis concluding that our forty-fifth president's "loosely woven sentences and cramped, simplistic vocabulary" placed his speech below a sixth-grade reading level (more than four reading levels behind his opponents' talking styles). A different study found that 78 percent of Trump's vocabulary was made up of monosyllabic words, and that his most frequently used lexical items included (in the following order) *I*, *Trump*, *very*, *China*, and *money*.

Those reports aren't exactly flattering; then again, it's not as if the folks likening Clinton's laugh to a witch were conducting empirical studies. Not to mention, there are countless men in power besides Trump—men whose eccentric speech styles are surely worth a look (Bernie Sanders, Bill Maher, Jon Stewart, John Oliver)— who have largely escaped the careful attention paid to so many female public figures. (And when attention is paid, it's often in the form of praise for their "passionate" delivery.)

The subject of attention leads to the fundamental reason why Clinton's and Thatcher's voices are as repellent to many listeners as Scarlett Johansson's is sexy. Quite simply, it's because female public figures are judged by their bodies, fashion, and overall sex appeal significantly more than their male colleagues. Calling Clinton "shrill" is motivated by the same thing as criticizing her "cankles"—another of the press's favorite digs from before she made the permanent switch to pantsuits. (Who knew a two-inch section of lower-leg flesh could be so newsworthy?) I would challenge you to find a male politician who has 20,500 Google search results dedicated to his cankles, but I've already tried it, and it was not an efficient use of my Wednesday afternoon.

What you also won't find, no matter how many press clippings you analyze, is language describing male authority figures' speech using sexual metaphors; meanwhile, you will find scores of sexual comparisons for powerful women. Cameron analyzed media commentary of the 2016 UK general election and was amazed by how often women politicians (and even debate moderators) were likened to archetypal female "battle-axes," like the austere headmistress of an all-girls' school or the vicious nurse in *One Flew Over the Cuckoo's Nest*. What these figures share is that they are all "aging, usually ugly, and either totally sexless or sexually voracious, terrifying the male objects of their insatiable desire," says Cameron.

To the contrary, we also have the velvety voices of the women from *BroBible*'s countdown: Scarlett Johansson, Charlize Theron, Penélope Cruz. These voices are whispery, never loud; low, never shrieking; and often peppered with the titillating lisps and long vowels of foreign tongues. And, most important, they belong to people who do not wish to be presidents or CEOs, but are

wordslut

instead just there for our entertainment. If these women were to run for public office, rest assured they would be slammed for not sounding authoritative enough. As proof, we can look to Welsh politician Leanne Wood, who has a soft, mellifluous timbre that Scottish Twitter pundit @AngryScotland once described as "audio chocolate"; at the same time, as Cameron recounts, her voice has been "endlessly patronized by the media." The voices of ScarJo, Charlize, and Penélope would surely not be deemed White House appropriate either—but at least they would never, heaven forbid, come across as unfuckable.

Critiques on both sides of the double bind are a means of linguistic objectification. As long as it remains strange for women to fill positions of authority, then we can expect their clothes, bodies, voices, and gender itself to be inevitably ogled. Until then, they will be forced to walk the tightrope of the double bind, careful not to slip and fall into either the box labeled "adorable eye candy" or the one marked "abrasive scold."

I asked Deborah Cameron for her advice on how ambitious women can navigate the double bind, how we can refocus the public's attention from the shrillness or sexiness of a woman's voice to what she's actually saying. She had a pretty good idea of what *doesn't* work: "It seems to me (sad irony) that women who think about it a lot and try hard to fix it (think: Clinton on the campaign trail, resisting the perception of her as aggressive by forcing herself to smile and not get angry when

Trump was baiting her) are often judged even more negatively than women who don't seem as concerned about impression management (Michelle Obama, Scotland's Nicola Sturgeon, Angela Merkel)."

Appearing genuine feels so essential to contemporary, internet-savvy audiences. Social media and round-the-clock press have caused relatability to become more important to the average consumer than competence. While working at a digital media company in the late 2010s, I regularly heard higher-ups use the phrase "authenticity over content" to describe the evolving tastes of a Twitter and YouTube–obsessed viewership. If Margaret Thatcher and her deep, heavily trained voice were to run for office now, Twitter would no doubt have a field day scorning her phoniness. As Cameron says, "Once you start listening to the spin doctors and the life coaches and trying to come across as more this and less that, you also come across as 'inauthentic.'" So if the pundits, trolls, and disgruntled employees are going to bust your chops either way, you might as well just be yourself.

At a time during her 2008 campaign when she was plummeting in the polls so epically that most people would have long since given up, Hillary Clinton made headlines after publicly crying on a trip to New Hampshire. It happened while she was answering an undecided voter's question about what makes her "get out the door every day," especially "as a woman." At first, Clinton chuckled the question off, but then her tone shifted. "This is very personal for me. Not just political. I see what's happening. We have to reverse it." As she said this, her eyes welled up and her voice cracked. "Some people think elections are a game: who's up or who's down. It's about our country. It's about our kids' futures. It's about all of us together."

This display of emotion was genuine, the public could tell ("I wanted to see who the real Hillary was. That was real," another undecided voter commented), and in the weeks following the episode, Clinton's rating went up. Obviously, it wasn't enough to help her win the New Hampshire primary, and some commentators thought her tears were too little too late. The catch-22, of course, is that it was Hillary's toughness and emotional resilience, the very qualities that painted her as a coldhearted shrew, that put her on that campaign trail in the first place.

There are successful women who seem to have navigated the linguistic double bind more smoothly than Clinton. According to a small poll I took among my social media followers, Senator Kamala Harris, Oprah Winfrey, TV broadcasters Diane Sawyer and Robin Roberts, and Sheryl Sandberg have all done a pretty bang-up job of striking a nice equilibrium, alongside Michelle Obama and Angela Merkel.

Even if every woman in power were to modulate her voice to perfection, managing to come across as balanced and worthy as the Winfreys of the world, it still wouldn't solve everything. After all, our bias against how women leaders sound is structural, not individual. The real solution is a long-term one.

In one of her 2015 columns for the *New York Times*, Sheryl Sandberg wrote that "the long-term solution to the double bind of speaking while female" is simple: we need to pick more women to be the boss. As we've already learned, adding women to workplace environments doesn't automatically earn them more respect; sometimes, it can even have the opposite effect by intimidating their male colleagues, impelling them to behave even more dominantly. However, when women make up the active *majority* of higher-up positions (or all of them), that story changes. Take it from University of Texas professor Ethan Burris, who studied a credit union staff made up of 74 percent women supervisors. "Sure enough," Sandberg reports, "when women spoke up there, they were more likely to be heard than men." Studies also show that by and large, companies led by women over-perform. "Start-ups led by women are more likely to succeed," Sandberg says, "innovative firms with more women in top management are more profitable; and companies with more gender diversity have more revenue, customers, market share, and profits."

Eventually, the more normal it is for women to lead and for men to follow—the more balanced the scales become—then there will be no such thing as a woman sounding "shrill" or "abrasive," because we will no longer automatically associate women with subservience. There will no longer be such a grotesque misalignment between what any given gender should sound like and what power should sound like. As sociolinguist Bonnie

McElhinny once wrote, "The more we allow men and women into one another's spheres and allow them to exhibit behaviors normatively understood as 'masculine' or 'feminine,' the more we will denaturalize and, in fact, redefine these understandings of gender."

While we're hiring a bunch of women to run the world, I recommend hiring a bunch of gay people too. Because if our whack ideas about how women speak are keeping us from living our best lives, you don't even want to know what we're missing when it comes to the mind-blowing world of queer language.

Actually, you do. You really, really do . . .

time to make this book just a little bit gayer

9

AND GLORIA CACKLED,
LET THERE BE SPARKLE:
AND THERE WAS SPARKLE.

—THE KING JAMES BIBLE,
TRANSLATED INTO POLARI

David Thorpe is embarrassed of his *s*'s.

He's embarrassed of his *o*'s, his *a*'s, and most of his other vowels too. He thinks the way he pronounces them makes him sound gay. Thorpe, an otherwise proud gay man himself, is a journalist, and like most reporters plagued by a needling question, he can't help but investigate the mystery of why the gay voice exists—and why he was beset with such an extreme case—by way of a 2014 documentary called *Do I Sound Gay?* In the film's opening scene, Thorpe presents a microphone to a series of strangers on the streets of New York City and poses the very question reflected in his movie's title: "Hello, sorry to bother you, I'm David Thorpe, and I have a question . . . do I sound gay?"

Thorpe is hoping his various subjects will say that he *doesn't* sound gay, but most of them tell him yes, he does, citing his "gay lisp," nasality, and singsongy intonation as proof. Thorpe isn't the only gay man who doesn't want to sound like it. "Do you think *you* sound gay?" he asks one guy with a yellow stud earring on what looks to be a corner of Manhattan's Chelsea neighborhood. "I hope not," the man says.

A year after *Do I Sound Gay?* is released, a video is uploaded to YouTube called "Do You Sound Like a Lesbian?" Similarly, a host, this time a woman in her twenties named Taylor, invites Los Angeles passersby to listen to a lineup of half a dozen young women as they each repeat the same stereotypically lesbian phrases— "My favorite store is Home Depot" and "I never leave the house without ChapStick." (They do this with irony, of course.) Then she asks her passersby to guess, based on the sound of the speakers' voices, which of the six is a lesbian.

These interviewees are far less confident in their answers than David Thorpe's. Most of them are unable to identify with any certainty which woman in the bunch talks like a lesbian, or flat-out refuse to try. Even the listeners that do wager a guess don't provide evidence as specific as nasality or lipsy *s*'s. One man says he senses a little "anger" in one of the women's voices. Three others base their guesses on the observation that a speaker stated her phrase "boldly" or with a "take-charge" or "assertive" delivery. "Ah, and [assertiveness] translates as gay to you," Taylor confirms with a fellow in a striped button-down. "It's out of the ordinary," he clarifies. "So, confidence for women is out of the ordinary," Taylor affirms. The guy blinks at her nervously.

As it turns out, all six of the women in Taylor's lineup identify as lesbians, which she ultimately reveals to her guessers, putting them out of their awkward misery. "I wouldn't have known," admits a young guy with curly brown hair. "I'm surprised about her, I'm surprised about her, I'm surprised about her too," agrees an older man in a bowler hat, as he points to a few women down the line. "So no chance for guys like us?"

The main difference between Taylor's survey and David Thorpe's is that the lesbian speakers aren't relieved that their speech doesn't seem to reflect their sexual orientation. "We *like* to affirm our queerness," one woman says. Another agrees: "We're not offended by [the idea of someone thinking we sound like lesbians]. We're not bummed about it."

The idea that you could identify someone's sexual

time to make this book just a little bit gayer

preference by how their voice sounds is objectively non-sensical (we don't copulate with our vocal cords, after all). So it makes some amount of common sense that not a single player in Taylor's "Do You Sound Like a Lesbian?" video was able to pass her test. What's more curious is that when David Thorpe posed the idea of the gay *male* voice to his subjects, they all knew (or at least felt like they knew) exactly what he was talking about.

As we've learned many times so far, almost every facet of human speech, down to the very languages we use and oftentimes even our pitch, is a product of nurture, not nature. Nobody comes out of the womb with a genetic predisposition to speaking with a singsongy intonation, and linguists have found absolutely zero correlation between homosexuality and a propensity to lisp your *s*'s. Some languages don't even have *s* consonants at all. Yet so many English speakers have the impression that a singular, recognizable "gay voice" exists, but don't recognize a lesbian equivalent.

My first awareness of the "gay male voice" arose in the sixth grade, when my best friend, a boy from my drama class, broke down crying one day after having endured an afternoon of bullying for how he pronounced his *s*'s. "They said I have a lisp," he told me. "They called me a homo."

Personally, I couldn't hear anything different about my friend's *s* pronunciation—it definitely didn't sound like he lisped—but in retrospect, I realize what his tormentors were talking about. As it turns out, the "gay male voice" that David Thorpe, his street interviewees, and many other English speakers seem to recognize is indeed a systematic phenomenon. Phoneticians (people who specialize in the study of speech sounds) have been able to describe the sound variations comprising this "gay voice": they include clearer, longer vowels; prolonged *s* and *z* sounds; a nasal vocal quality; and an over-articulation of *t*'s, *p*'s, and *k*'s (this is when you release a little puff of air after a consonant-final word, like *cat* or *thick*, almost so it sounds like "cat-*uh*" or "thick-*uh*"). Scholars have also noticed that upspeak and a swoopy, musical inflection are features of this so-called gay male voice. And then of course there is what's commonly known as the "gay lisp," which, as it turns out, is not a lisp at all.

In the spirit of vindicating my middle school friend, I want to clear the air about the "gay lisp" right now: A *real* lisp is a phonological delay usually found in children's speech that's caused when one pushes their tongue too far forward in the mouth, resulting in an "s" pronunciation that sounds more like a "th." (Think of Cindy from *The Brady Bunch*: "They *ttthhhay* I talk like a baby!") But the *s* that we might identify as "sounding gay" is not in fact a lisp; instead, it's what linguists classify as a sibilant *s*, and it's produced by placing the tip of the tongue on the roof of the mouth so that a sort of whistling noise results. Speech scientists guarantee there is absolutely zero evidence that gay men are likelier to lisp, but that in decades past, young boys who spoke with sibilant *s*'s were often mischaracterized as having a lisp and sent to speech therapy to fix it. "There was a lot of confusion back then," explains University of Texas language scholar Ron Smyth, "between a fronted 'th' sound and just sounding too feminine."

The concept of a man "sounding too feminine" is an important piece in the puzzle of where the gay male voice comes from and why it causes folks like David Thorpe and my middle school friend such grief. As you may have noticed, many of these gay speech variations are similar to the elements first identified by Robin Lakoff in the 1970s: upspeak, an over-articulation of plosive consonants, and a swoopy inflection are also stereotypes of how women talk.

We already know that not all women speak with these features, and it's also not only women who use them. The same logic can be applied to gay men. Just as there are plenty of men who use tag questions and vocal fry, there are plenty of straight guys who have nasal, sing-songy voices; and equally, there are plenty of gay men who "sound straight."

Smyth argues that how feminine or masculine our vocal affects sound might have to do with the speech of the communities in which we grow up. In *Do I Sound Gay?* Thorpe introduces a straight friend of his who was raised on an ashram surrounded by mostly women and now sounds stereotypically gay (his voice is "all treble, no bass,"* the guy explains with a smile and one of the

---

* Actually, pitch is not really a variable in the gay voice equation. As long as you speak with nasality, sibilant *s*'s, and upspeak, you can "sound

most sibilant *s*'s I've ever heard). Meanwhile, another one of Thorpe's friends, who is indeed gay, grew up in a family of jock brothers and now talks like your average heterosexual, football-loving bro (low monotone pitch, extensive sports vocabulary).

Scholars argue that many gay men might unconsciously "learn" the gay voice not only from their communities but also from TV and movies. Since the nineteenth century, gay male characters have had a place in mainstream American entertainment; it's just that until the 1990s or so they were always in the form of some extreme stereotype, like the wealthy, foppish "pansy" or the hyperintellectual cunning villain. In *Do I Sound Gay?* David Thorpe explains that growing up, he didn't have any gay figures to relate to in his community (at least none that were out),* but he knew what gay men sounded like because of a few on-screen archetypes. These included Liberace and Truman Capote, with their nasally affects, as well as sophisticated movie villains like Waldo Lydecker

gay" whether you have a voice as high as that of the writer David Sedaris (who often complains of being mistaken for a woman on the phone) or as deep as that of *Project Runway*'s Tim Gunn (who, despite his rich bass, told David Thorpe that the first time he heard his voice on TV, he was "appalled").

* You might have heard people from small towns, or people from older generations, claim that "no one sounded gay" where they grew up. University of Minnesota linguist Benjamin Munson has a pretty reasonable explanation for this, which is that in a more conservative place or time period, it might have been so taboo to be gay that listeners didn't even allow their minds to entertain the idea, no matter how many sibilant *s*'s were tossed around. It could also be true that in less cosmopolitan areas, there simply wasn't enough of a gay culture for anyone to know what the "gay voice" sounded like in the first place. Thus, no one learned it, used it, or heard it.

in 1944's *Laura* and Addison DeWitt in 1950's *All About Eve*, both portrayed as impeccably dressed, acid-tongued dandies.

Characters like Lydecker and DeWitt contributed to the stereotype that to be educated and refined was to be gay, and to be gay was to be evil. This notion went so far that the villains in many Disney movies were painted as pretentious gay men: think of Captain Hook and Jafar with their flamboyant hats and aristocratic airs, not to mention Ursula the Sea Witch, who was openly inspired by the iconic drag queen Divine. Even Disney's badly behaved animals, like Shere Khan, Scar, and Professor Ratigan from *The Great Mouse Detective*, were characterized as soft-handed homosexuals, all assigned the same vaguely British accents, bombastic vocabularies, and disdain for working-class stupidity ("I'm surrounded by idiots" is one of Scar's famous lines).

With the help of these characters, an effeminate, learned style of speech became a symbol of the gay community and something that its members could learn and teach each other. It's a dialect of sorts, which one can drop into or camp up whenever the situation calls for it. This is called "code switching," and sexuality aside it's actually something almost all English speakers do. Most of us speak more than one dialect of English, which we might learn from our ethnic community, the geographic region where we grow up, or a new region we transplant to (think of, say, a native Texan living in Los Angeles who speaks Standard English around Californians, but drops into their hometown accent the second they're around other Texans). Consciously or unconsciously, we all adjust our codes depending on the context of the conversation. This is an incredibly useful tool, because it helps us better connect to the people we're talking to.

The male "gay voice" that David Thorpe and his interviewees were referencing does not represent the entire gay community, but instead just a small part of it—the white and cosmopolitan part. And it's a code that people outside that community can drop into when the situation calls for it, as well. A good example of how this type of code switching can work comes from a group of first-generation American Latino gay men in a Southern California town outside Los Angeles. According to a 2012 study by Cal Poly scholar Anthony C. Ocampo, these men didn't speak with the white cosmopolitan "gay voice" at home because it didn't meet the masculinity standards of their families. As American-born Latino sons of immigrants, these guys possessed a very strong ethnic identity, but a rather ambivalent sexual one, because the effeminate characteristics of nearby white gay Los Angeles, which weren't accepted in their home communities, didn't match their macho presentation, which, on the flip side, was stigmatized in West Hollywood.

While with their families, these guys would speak a masculine, more "straight sounding" form of English (or Spanish). Among other gay Latino men from similar backgrounds, their speech styles and vocabularies remained fairly macho—playful insults, boasting about their sexual conquests (in this community, "manning up" to the fact that they wanted to have sex with other men was actually seen as the masculine thing to do and thus more highly valued than hiding or denying it). It wasn't until these men physically immersed themselves in the scene of white gay Los Angeles that they would code switch into the more feminine style, like using sibilant *s*'s and gender-inverted pronouns (aka calling each other *she* or *girl*). They were able to do this knowing that in the West Hollywood environment, their masculinity would not be questioned.

If you're a person who code switches a lot, it's possible to forget what your most natural speech sounds like. One speech pathologist suspected this might be what happened with David Thorpe, who has been pronouncing his *s*'s and vowels like his white gay community in New York City for so long that, to his frustration, he finds it almost impossible to switch back.

So the "gay voice," if you want to call it that, does exist—it's just that not all gay men of every background and ethnicity use it, those who do don't necessarily use it all the time, and not everyone who happens to use it is gay. In fact, one of Smyth's studies revealed that listeners could correctly identify a man's sexual orientation by his voice with only 60 percent accuracy. The cultural stereotype that all gay men naturally talk like women is as precarious as the stereotype that all women naturally use uptalk and prefer to gossip about people instead of debating ideas. It's just . . . not that simple.

Our culture *wants* it to be that simple—to believe so
badly that all gay men sound like women—because that
makes it easier to size them up and potentially ridicule
them. Thus, the stereotype prevails. "Why do you think
gay men sometimes reject other gay men for sounding
gay?" David Thorpe asks gay media pundit Dan Savage. "Misogyny," Savage responds. "They want to prove
to the culture that they're not *not* men—that they're
good because they're not women. . . . And then they
punish gay men who they perceive as being feminine in
any way."

Ultimately, when it comes to how a gay man talks,
any shame experienced results from the fact that this
speech style defies our expectations of how a man should
sound. Meanwhile, not one of the lesbians in Taylor's
lineup was sent to a speech pathologist for sounding
too "assertive."

There have been a few linguists over the years who've
tried to identify a lesbian voice equivalent to the gay
male one. But they haven't been able to find much. And
by "much," I mean anything at all. In 1997 Stanford
University phonologist Arnold Zwicky proposed that
the "nonexistence" of a lesbian speech style might be
perceived because gay men who use the proverbial
"voice" are, whether they realize it or not, signaling a desire to remove themselves from normative, heterosexual
masculinity. Lesbians, on the other hand, more often
identify closely *with* their gender group, not against
it, so they don't share the same need to differentiate

themselves from straight women. By Zwicky's thinking, lesbians are women first, gay women second, whereas gay men go the other way around.

I love the idea that lesbian women have such strong gender solidarity (because women are the best, *duh*). However, asking, "Why is there no lesbian equivalent of the gay male voice?" isn't the right question to begin with. That's because this question treats the gay male experience as the standard to which the lesbian experience should be compared, instead of looking at the lesbian experience as its own separate thing.

Any social group's language is a direct product of its history. Because gay men and lesbians do not have parallel histories, their language necessarily couldn't be the same. Just look at the evolution of each community's portrayal in the media: until shockingly recently, lesbian characters were entirely missing from American TV and cinema. And when they did finally appear, it was not in a positive light. One of first major lesbian story lines surfaced in the 1961 film *The Children's Hour*, which tells the story of a disgruntled boarding school student who accuses her two headmistresses of being in a romantic relationship, ultimately ruining their personal and professional reputations forever. This movie didn't make a comment on lesbian speech specifically, but it certainly portrayed lesbian life as dark, lonely, and career-ruining.

A slightly better question to ask, then, and the one

that Zwicky seemed to be getting at, was why gay men seem to adopt linguistic features stereotypically associated with women, while lesbians don't seem to do the same in the opposite direction? Why do gay men engage in gender inversion, but not gay women?

The answer is simple: it's not that lesbians *don't* speak in a masculine way; it's just that it's not as abhorrent for women to talk like men as it is for men to talk like women. "Because who wants to be female?" our NYU linguist Louise O. Vasvári asked me facetiously over the phone. "A male who wants to be female is the ultimate downgrade."

This perceived downgrade is yet another example of our cultural view that masculine language is the neutral, unmarked default, whereas femininity represents otherness. Switching from a default position to a marked position is more noticeable than the reverse, so when a man opens his mouth and "feminine" traits come out, we flinch. "You can go toward power, but if you're a man who chooses to be female sounding, you're moving away from it, and that's a negative," says Vasvári, following up with this analogy: "I look at my classrooms and how many of the female students are wearing pants? Most of them. How many men are wearing skirts? None."

Just like a man wearing a skirt makes a bolder social statement than a woman wearing pants, a man speaking like a woman makes a bolder statement than a woman speaking like a man. Certainly, it's possible for a woman to go *too* far: Hillary Clinton and Margaret Thatcher's "abrasive" voices might be the equivalent of a woman, say, wearing a boxy tuxedo and no makeup to a black-tie event. A woman would have to take her gender inversion much further than a man for anyone to notice.

The inequity between gay and lesbian speech doesn't stop at the voice. We have different impressions of each community's slang too. For decades, language scholars have documented the vivid slang vocabularies of gay men in various communities around the world. In the Philippines, many gay men use a lexicon called *swardspeak*, which combines imaginative wordplay, pop culture references, malapropisms (word misusages), and onomatopoeia (words that sound like what they mean, like *clink* and *swoosh*). For example, in swardspeak, *Muriah Carrey* means "cheap" and is derived from the Tagalog word *mura*, which means the same thing, combined with the name of gay pop icon Mariah Carey. There's also *taroosh*, a take on the Tagalog *taray*, which means "bitchy." (Adding an *oosh* suffix to a word to make it cuter is a classic characteristic of swardspeak.)

In English, the first major glossary of gay slang was written in 1941 by American folklorist and student of literary erotica Gershon Legman. It appeared as an appendix to a two-volume medical study of homosexuality that featured everything from case studies of sphincter tightness to X-rays of lesbian pelvic areas (scientist, pervert . . . tomato, *to-mah-to*). This appendix listed precisely 329 items, some of which I have never seen (take *sister in distress*, meaning, "a homosexual male in trouble, usually with the police" or *church mouse*: a homosexual who frequents churches and cathedrals in order to cruise pious young men) and others that definitely ring a bell (like *fish*, which refers to a homosexual man who is very feminine—*fish* is a somewhat problematic metaphor used to describe vaginas).

It did not slip past Legman that most of these terms were male oriented. The lack of lesbian slang was, as he wrote, "very noticeable." Legman postulated that perhaps this slang disparity was due to the fact that female homosexuality simply didn't exist. Being interested in women was, by his measure, just a hobby for flighty rich girls who were either bored, faking it, or severely repressed by the men in their lives. "Lesbianism in America—and perhaps elsewhere—seems in a large measure factitious," Legman wrote, "a faddish vice among the intelligentsia, a good avenue of entry in the theatre, and most of all, a safe resource for timid women and demi-virgins, an erotic outlet for the psychosexually traumatised daughters of tyrannous fathers and a despairing retreat for the wives and ex-wives of clumsy, brutal or ineffectual lovers." None of that, he suggested, lent itself to good slang.

This may sound like the thinking of a sexist jerk, but there are real factors that might have led Legman to his conclusions. One is that before LGBTQ+ liberation in the 1960s and '70s, gay men were much more likely to be arrested and imprisoned for their sexuality than lesbians were. "Homosexual acts" (mostly meaning sodomy) were illegal in the majority of English-speaking countries through most of the twentieth century. In Scotland, for example, the ban on anal sex between men was not officially lifted until 2013. The heightened risk that came with being a gay male could have elevated the need for an exclusive vocabulary with which to communicate in public. It protected gay men and also strengthened their solidarity.

"Even the word *gay* is an example," American University linguist William Leap told me, referencing a time in mid-twentieth-century America when most mainstream speakers still recognized the word *gay* to mean "happy." By asking someone in public, "Do you know any gay places around here?" gay men could identify who was a part of their community and who could be trusted. There are dozens of other undercover code words like this, dating back decades. I try to keep a straight face as Leap tells me about another popular metaphor once used by gay men to pinpoint others—"I adore seafood, but I can't stand fish"—which can be found in documents as old as the 1940s.

Some of the most persecuted queer communities in English-speaking history are in fact responsible for much of mainstream culture's best slang. You might be familiar with terms like *throwing shade* (meaning, "to insult"), *werk* (an expression of praise), and *slay* (to do something very well), which are just a handful of the beloved twenty-first-century slang words that originated in black and Latinx* ballroom culture.

Ballroom culture, from which so many beloved English slang terms originate, centers around drag competitions whose heyday was in 1980s Harlem, New York. These were events where gay and trans performers of color could dress in fabulous feminine clothing, walk the runway, and find close community and acceptance, which they were often missing from the families they were born into. So much amazing pop culture originated in the ballroom scene, including the vogue style of dance (no, it didn't come from Madonna), plus treasured slang terms like *werk*, *read*, *face beat*, *hunty*, *extra*, *gagging*, *serving realness*, *tea*, *kiki*, and *yas*, which, as of the time I'm writing this book, have become so commonly used, especially on the internet, that many folks think they were invented there.

Canadian linguist Gretchen McCulloch can explain the difference between internet slang and slang that's simply used on the internet: true internet slang is language that came to be through the medium of typing via chat rooms, social media, and online games (think acronyms,

---

*   Latinx, by the way, is a term that's emerged as a gender-neutral alternative to Latino and Latina. The *Huffington Post*'s "Latino Voices" column considers the word "part of a 'linguistic revolution' that aims to move beyond gender binaries and is inclusive of the intersecting identities of Latin American descendants." Not everyone is in love with *Latinx* (for one, it doesn't exactly roll off the tongue while you're speaking Spanish), but again, gender-neutral language is an ongoing conversation, and this is what's in use at the time I'm writing this.

emoji, hashtags, typos, memes, digital terminology), and it inherently could not exist before or without the internet. To say something like "*Lol, unsubscribe*" or "*Tbh, he's even a troll IRL*"—and certainly to type something like *tl;dr*, *NSFW*, *asdfghjkl;*, or "you've been *pwned!*"—would be to employ genuine internet slang. But simply using a slang word on Reddit that already existed offline for decades technically does not make it internet lingo. After all, any slang that's widely used in real life is inevitably going to end up on the internet.

In an episode of the podcast *Reply All*, hosted by two straight white dudes in their thirties (which I happen to like very much despite these shortcomings), the guys were very confidently explaining that the slang word *yas* originated on Twitter as an enthusiastic take on the word *yes* and was popularized thanks to the television show *Broad City*. Upon hearing this, many of their listeners (myself included) had a teeny-weeny aneurysm. Because *yas* is not nerdy white-people Twitter slang. Not even close.

Reply All's audience quickly called them on their mistake about the origins of *yas*, and in the following episode, a performer who was active in the 1980s ballroom scene named Jose Xtravaganza was invited on the show. Xtravaganza expressed that for the community that invented *yas*, the stakes were much higher than appearing hip online. It was a matter of survival—of banding together to cope with the bigotry they were faced with every day. "We were speaking code," he said.

"For no one else to understand. . . . For just us, you know? It was our code against society."

Sonja Lanehart has made the point that straight white (or even gay white) people using words like *yas* and *werk* to seem hip is sort of like white pop singers wearing dreadlocks, gold chains, and low-hanging jeans; it's an act of lifting the "cool" parts of an oppressed culture while conveniently leaving behind the things that make actually being a part of that culture, which invented the cool stuff in the first place, very hard.

Generously, Lanehart also says that straight white people don't have to stop saying "yas queen" just as Justin Bieber doesn't have to remove his jewelry; but if they are going to continue making use of the products of marginalized groups, then at the very least, they can recognize and support these communities in exchange. The ballroom collective House of Xtravaganza once summed up their position on the matter in a succinct Instagram post: "You can't be homophobic/transphobic and use terms such as 'yaaass' or 'giving me life' or 'werk' or 'throwing shade' or 'reading' or 'spilling tea.' These phrases are direct products of drag and ball culture. You don't get to dehumanize black and Latinx queer/trans people and then appropriate our shit."

There are other English-speaking countries whose queer communities are responsible for their best slang. Another robust gay vocabulary comes from British English: it's called Polari. During the early to mid-twentieth century, many gay men in Britain were fluent in this form of cant slang (that's a lexicon created explicitly to deceive or confuse outsiders). Used as early as the 1500s, Polari—an iteration of the Italian verb *parlare*, meaning "to speak"—was an eclectic mix of London slang, words pronounced backward, and broken Romani, Yiddish, and Italian. The vocabulary contained several hundred words, and if you knew what to listen for, you could hear them among everyone from actors and circus performers to wrestlers and navy sailors to members of various gay subcultures. But to everyone else, it sounded like gobbledygook. That was the whole idea.

Polari culture is really only remembered by those who were there during its peak in the 1950s and '60s. I was able to find a couple YouTube clips of its speakers; in one, a seventy-six-year-old former drag performer named Stan Murano lists his best-loved terms from back in the day: "If we saw a nice looking man, we'd say 'bona ro me, dear.' . . . Your fingers were your *martinis*; your bum, they called that your *brandygage* . . . your *ogles* were your eyes, hair was your *riah* . . . your shoes were your *bats*." He smiles as he reminisces.

Polari became less of a secret in the mid-1960s due to a popular BBC radio show that featured a couple of Polari-speaking characters (don't you just hate it when mainstream media ruins your favorite underground cant slang?). And after homosexuality was decriminalized in Britain in 1967, gay liberationist activists, who saw the lingo as politically regressive, discouraged people from using it. Still, several Polari words can be found in modern British (and sometimes American) slang, including *bear* (a large, hairy gay man), *twink* (a young gay man with no body hair), *bumming* (anal sex), *cottaging* (cruising for sex in public bathrooms), *camp* (effeminate), *trade* (sexual partner), and *fantabulous* (self-explanatory).

Lesbian slang, by contrast, doesn't have a history as rich as that of ballroom slang or Polari. Or at least it doesn't have nearly as strong a record. There are two main reasons for the lack of documentation on lesbian language: First, there's the fact that even though gay women were less likely to be arrested pre-LGBTQ+ liberation, it was also extremely hard for them to live independently of men, and that made it more difficult to develop an extensive, widely known lexicon. Simply put, society made it trickier for lesbians to find each other in the first place. (Another possible reason why Gershon Legman didn't believe they existed at all.) As lesbian feminist linguist Julia Penelope once explained, "Lesbians have been socially and historically invisible in our society and isolated from one another as a consequence." For this reason, they didn't have the chance to build a "cohesive community in which a lesbian aesthetic could have developed," Penelope says.

At the same time, we know that lesbian slang in the pre-LGBTQ+ liberation era definitely did exist. We're sure of this in part because of a social scientist named Rose Giallombardo, who published a 1966 study of women's prisons, part of which involved examining a number of letters exchanged by female inmates in romantic relationships. (One thing she found was that a lot of the slang used in these letters revolved around the butch/femme role dynamic. Butches, also known as *studs*, *kings*, and *mantees*, fulfilled a dominant role; femmes were submissive.)

Generally speaking, slang thrives in what some sociologists term "total institutions," which have historically been sex-segregated: prisons, the army, summer camps, boarding schools. In decades past, researchers like Legman didn't exactly perceive women's prisons as hotbeds of linguistic discovery. (Plus, they didn't have easy access to such places.) So the lesbian slang at which Giallombardo got a small peek in the 1960s was largely missed.

Even though vocabularies like lesbian gender role terminology, Polari, swardspeak, and ballroom slang exist (or did once), just like the gay voice, it's not as if *all* gay people use or even know about them. After all, LGBTQ+ folks come from a near infinite number of different geographic, racial, educational, and socioeconomic backgrounds, and not all of them would even have access to the language of these individual subcultures. In the mid-1970s, a team of researchers looked into gay men's knowledge of what was supposed to be "their" slang and found that plenty of them had never heard of the words at all. If people had cared to look into lesbian slang at the time, the same probably could have been said for them. That's likely even more true for gay women, whose history is marked by so much isolation.

In the age of the internet, and *especially* as ideas of sexual fluidity become more accepted, none of the language we've discussed in this chapter so far is really considered all that "gay" anymore. Deborah Cameron and another linguist named Don Kulick once said that rather than perceiving a sibilant *s* or gender pronoun inversion as descriptive of how gay people talk, it is instead more logical and productive to think of them as linguistic resources that are "available for anyone— regardless of their erotic orientation" to draw on in order to produce an effect. Think of all the gay icons that speak "like gay men" to create a certain persona, but aren't gay men themselves (Miss Piggy, Mae West). Or people like Oprah and Buffy the Vampire Slayer, who are regarded by some as queer icons for women, but aren't actually lesbians.

If this sounds like another example of LGBTQ+ communities losing their language to straight people, like in the case of attributing *yas* to Twitter, rest assured that it isn't. Instead, this is a case of leveling the linguistic playing field, so that "straight speech" no longer enjoys its default, unmarked status. After all, wouldn't it be better to live in a world where a man sounding like a woman is not only no longer a symbol of gayness or invitation for harassment, but isn't even an idea that crosses people's minds? Wouldn't it be better to live in a world where a woman sounding "angry" or "assertive" didn't necessarily make her a lesbian (and vice versa)?

In such a world, David Thorpe's sibilant *s*'s and Taylor's

"abrasive"-sounding subjects would only be considered "gay" if they consciously chose to camp these features up as a way to express some sort of statement or effect. And when they did, the idea of someone transgressing linguistic gender norms would be so accepted, so innocuous, that a listener would hear it and think, *Oh, this is a comment on gay identity, cool*, the same as they would think, *Oh, this is a comment on Midwest identity* upon hearing someone speak with a satirically over-the-top Chicago accent.

In 2012 two artists from Manchester collaborated with a Lancaster University linguist to launch an app called Polari Mission, which features a dictionary of more than five hundred Polari words, as well as—and whoever thought of this really deserves a prize—the King James Bible translated, from start to finish, into Polari. The document commences: "In the beginning Gloria created the heaven and the earth. . . . And the fairy of Gloria trolled upon the eke of the aquas. And Gloria cackled, Let there be sparkle: and there was sparkle."

I'm grateful that we no longer live in a world where this version of the Bible *needs* to exist, that we've come far enough that queer people don't have to use secret codes anymore to survive. But as a word geek, I find myself quite charmed that we have a record of it—proof that in the darkest times, language can offer people a creative and colorful safe haven.

Also, motion to bring back the verb *cackle* as a synonym for *say*. Dare I cackle, I'm a big, big fan.

cyclops, panty puppet, bald-headed bastard

(and 100+ other things to call your genitalia)

Jonathon Green has led a team of researchers on what is surely one of the most NSFW linguistic projects ever. After meticulously combing through several thousand books, newspapers, scripts, dictionaries, and other written documents dating back to the thirteenth century, Green, a British slang lexicographer, has amassed one of the most thorough and extensive catalogs of genitalia words in recorded history. Completed in 2013, the archive contains a total of 2,600 terms, both modern and antiquated, all meaning penis, vagina, balls, or some other unit of the human nether region. To put it in perspective, that's more entries than there were in the entire first English dictionary, total.

Green has created two separate time lines, divided by sex: his time line of penis and testicle nicknames in-

MEN'S AND WOMEN'S GENITALIA SLANG THROUGHOUT HISTORY

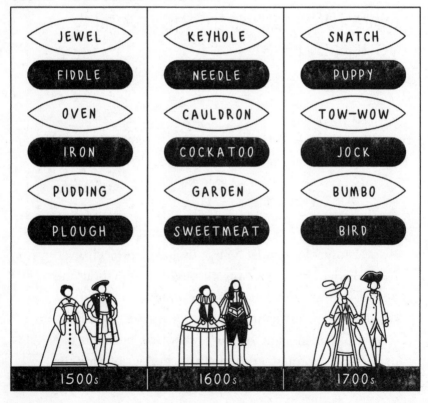

JEWEL	KEYHOLE	SNATCH
FIDDLE	NEEDLE	PUPPY
OVEN	CAULDRON	TOW-WOW
IRON	COCKATOO	JOCK
PUDDING	GARDEN	BUMBO
PLOUGH	SWEETMEAT	BIRD
1500s	1600s	1700s

cludes those as famous as *salami* and *nutsack*, and those as exotic as *diddlywhacker, butcher knife,* and *one-eyed trouser snake* (the latter three, by the way, come from the mid-1960s, and I challenge you to picture your father saying them without triggering your gag reflex). Green's vagina terms range from the well-known *beaver* and *snatch box* to the more colorful *carnal mantrap, cauldron, quim whiskers,* and *sweet potato pie.*

cyclops, panty puppet, bald-headed bastard

1800s	1900s	2000s
CLAM	JELLYROLL	MOOT
NOB	DINGBAT	JAMMER
TULIP	BOOGIE	BATCAVE
DINK	NARDS	OLD CHAP
OLD DING	WAZOO	BURGER
SCHLONG	LOVE PUMP	BONAPHONE

Twenty-six hundred genitalia terms is a lot—can you imagine if we had as many nicknames for your elbow? But in the centuries-old chronicle of English slang, genitalia words have always been one of its most resilient categories. Considering the innate taboo of these body parts, it makes sense that we'd come up with so many nicknames, metaphors, and euphemisms for them, and presumably people have been doing so since long before there was a record for Green to discover. Even the very first "private part" words we learn as kids are a form of euphemistic slang: *pee pee, hoo hoo, thingy* . . . whether it's out of shame, humor, sexiness, or a combination of the three, we just can't seem to stick to the classic *penis* and *vagina*.

Green did not accrue this data simply for fun—he was looking for patterns. Perhaps the most conspicuous one he found was how consistent, and how unsettling, the themes of our genitalia words have remained over time. As Green told reporters shortly after his study was published, "The penis is often going to be some kind of weapon, the vagina some kind of narrow passage, intercourse some way of saying 'man hits woman.'" The fact that these troubling metaphors have stuck around for so long is no accident. Linguists who specialize in the English vocabulary of "dirty talk" have determined that if you want to know something about our culture's mainstream attitudes toward sex—that it is penetrative by definition, that it's over as soon as the guy ejaculates, that men are horny pursuers while women are docile, undesiring objects—just look at the words we've come up with to describe it. The wince-worthy language we use to speak about sex is often a crystal-clear illustration of the disturbing ways we approach it in real life.

Among these decorated dirty-talk scholars is our Santa Barbara linguist Lal Zimman, who has spent years analyzing how folks of different genders use genitalia words to identify their own bodies and sexual experiences. "Overall it's really clear that the way we talk about genitals is a super concentrated representation of how we think about sex and gender," he tells me. "The research that people have done on heteronormative gender naming really shows that our worst cultural values are reflected in the ways we talk about genitals. Like penises are always weapons that exist for penetrating, sex is always violence, and women and vaginas are passive and absence, just a place to put a penis."

This phallus-centric perspective goes far beyond genitalia words. Just think of some of the most common verbs used to illustrate sex: *bone, drill, screw*. In the world of these words, the person with the erection is both the star and the narrator. If one were to describe sex from the vagina's standpoint—to say something like, "We *enveloped* all night," or "I *sheathed* the living daylights out of him," or "We *clitsmashed*"—it would be such an exceptional rebellion against mainstream sex talk that to many listeners, it would be a real head-scratcher.

These implications aren't exclusive to slang; they're embedded in official dictionary entries and medical

cyclops, panty puppet, bald-headed bastard

literature too. At the time I'm writing this, one of the definitions of *vagina* from TheFreeDictionary.com's medical glossary reads, "An organ of copulation that receives the penis during sexual intercourse." This is not a political view of the vagina, it's a medical one. And yet, I would invite a doctor to try telling a lesbian that her vagina is "an organ that receives the penis." See how well that goes.

Inspired by Jonathon Green's naughty time line—and genuinely curious to learn what genitalia words my personal friend group likes, uses, and avoids—I conducted a small-scale survey of my own. On Facebook, I asked people to message me lists of their favorite and least favorite genitalia terms, both technical and slang. (In retrospect, I probably should have been more judicious about my data collection method; some of the most enthusiastic answers came from my highly Facebook-active aunts, and let me tell you, having my parents' sisters tell me what they like to call their vaginas is probably one of the most uncomfortable research experiences I've ever had.)

In the end, I was able to gather genitalia terms from about twenty people, ages nineteen to sixty-three, both men and women, queer and straight. In addition to the classic *dick* and *cock*, their penis word lists included *dong, schlong, sausage, pickle, lollipop, prick, joystick, sword, staff, sniper rifle, pocket rocket, rod of pleasure, cyclops, torpedo,* and *anaconda*. Aside from good old *pussy* and *cunt*, vagina names included *va-jay-jay, vag, honey pot, snatch, clam, box, cave, garage, taco, ax wound, coochie, snake pit, beef curtains, meat wallet,* and *cum sponge.*

Interestingly, when it came to the vagina, I noticed that my non-straight female friends tended to prefer more explicit terms, like *pussy*, while my straight friends often went for PG nicknames—*va-jay-jay, vag.* I wondered if this might be because queer women are more comfortable with the vagina itself and possibly with female desire in general.

Personally, I'm inclined to think yes. Throughout my depressingly heterosexual teens and early twenties, I always felt perfectly chill about, even delighted by, our many slang terms for the penis—*dick, pickle, ding-dong,* even plain old *penis.* But I was never able to find a word for *vagina* that didn't make me squirm a little. I often defended my position with the argument that the word *vagina* itself is long, cumbersome, and lacks the plosive opening that makes *penis* so fun. Until I was seven, I actually pronounced the word "bagina" with a *b*, and when I discovered it actually started with a *v*, I suddenly liked it way less. Perhaps even my tiny self found that snappy *b* sound, the voiced sibling of the *p* in *penis*, more whimsical and inviting than the unwieldy *v*.

Realistically, though, I know my issue with *vagina* was more complicated than that. And I am far from the only person who's ever been put off by the word. Take it from Shonda Rhimes, creator of the hit TV series *Grey's Anatomy*, who once told *O, The Oprah Magazine* that in an early episode of *Grey's*, the word *penis* appeared thirty-two times and nobody blinked an eye, but when they tried to work *vagina* into the script just twice (and, again, this is a medical term), the higher-ups at broadcast standards objected.

This is actually the very reason why the word *va-jay-jay* was invented in the first place. Rhimes heard an assistant use it on the set of *Grey's* in the mid-2000s and instantly thought it was "the greatest phrase [she'd] ever heard." After it was written into the script, America fell in love with it overnight. Soon, *va-jay-jay* became the *vagina* alternative of choice for gynecologists, moms, even Oprah herself. ("And YOU get a *va-jay-jay*, and YOU get a *va-jay-jay*!")

I think part of what people loved about *va-jay-jay* was that, unlike so many other slang words for the vagina, this one was female-invented and felt like it belonged to women. Plus, the sound of the word was friendlier than *vagina* (and certainly friendlier than something like *cunt* or *twat*). That repetition of *jay-jay* is reminiscent of baby language, like *goo goo*, *ga ga*, and *hoo hoo*. It made it sound cuter and more welcoming—"it" being both the word itself and the general concept of female sexuality, which has a long history of censorship, linguistic and otherwise.*

---

* The on-screen depiction of oral sex performed on women has consistently earned movies an NC-17 rating—*Blue Valentine*, *Boys Don't Cry*, and *Charlie Countryman* are a few that come to mind. The same standard has certainly not been applied to on-screen blow jobs. I often think of 2013's *Lovelace*, a biopic about the star of the 1972 porn film *Deep Throat*. This

All that said, there is technically nothing scary about the word *vagina* itself. Most of the replacements our language offers are much more frightening: *ax wound, snake pit, beef curtains.* These sound like something out of *The Texas Chainsaw Massacre.* And it's not like the more passive alternatives are much better—*box, cave, garage.* I don't know about you, but my *va-jay-jay* is not just some lonely, empty pit waiting for a rod of pleasure to come fulfill its purpose. Adorable, friendly *va-jay-jay* doesn't actually do it for me, either. After all, why must the idea of female sexuality only be palatable when it's branded as cute? Not to mention, technically, the vagina is just the space connecting the uterus to the outside world—the canal itself, the "place to put a penis." The vulva's erogenous zones (the G-spot, the clitoris) aren't even a part of how we refer to women's genitalia at all.

When it comes to the language of sex, our dick-centrism is so deeply ingrained that most people's interpretation of the word *fuck* inherently involves a penis, even though the term itself does not actually suggest one. Before the fifteenth century, "to fuck" meant "to strike," which has intense physical implications, sure, but not necessarily phallic ones. As a queer friend of mine named Molly once put it, our penile associations with *fuck* exist only because "people think you can't fuck without a dick. Like lady sex is dainty

cyclops, panty puppet, bald-headed bastard

---

was an entire movie dedicated to fellatio, and to extreme sexual violence, and even that was given a mild R. Sure, let the kids watch a porn star get repeatedly raped, but female desire? No, no, no.

and not real because there's no man. Cisgender man on cisgender man sex? Real sex. Vagina on vagina sex? Not really real. I've totally been told by men that I can't ever be fucked by a woman, which is so laughable to me that I don't even get riled up about it."

All things considered, it is really no wonder that having grown up under the impression that a vagina is nothing but a vacant receptacle for a penis—a *cum sponge*, as it were—it takes most people who have vaginas decades (if they ever figure it out) to learn how to shtup* in a way that's fun and satisfying, and not boring, depressing, or an unspoken mystery.

There are linguists who've tried to understand where the language of our contemporary sex education went so wrong. Among them is a pair of scholars named Lisa Bland and Rusty Barrett (quirky names, quirky research), who broached the topic in a 1998 examination of sex advice from a handful of best-selling self-help books. A key topic in the books they investigated was teaching primarily heterosexual women how to "talk dirty" as a way of improving their experiences in bed. The authors of these books spent a lot of time urging women to get over the "guilt" of using "taboo words" by, for example, paying attention to the dialogue in porn, calling phone sex operators, and reading romance novels out loud.

A woman named Barbara Keesling authored a 1996

---

* This is one of my personal favorite synonyms for sex. It comes on loan from the Yiddish word meaning "to push," and has been employed by wordy American Jews like myself since the mid-1960s.

book titled *Talk Sexy to the One You Love*, and in it she urges her readers to make written lists of sexy terms and practice saying them aloud. "Now, in the lowest of whispers, whisper the word 'penis,'" she writes. "Whisper it again and again and again. Keep your eyes closed and keep thinking about your lover's penis. . . . Whisper the word a little louder. Louder still. . . . Repeat this process for all of the words and phrases on your 'penis' list." Next, she teaches her readers how to work these words into coherent conversation. "Sexy nouns can certainly spice up a sentence," she writes, "but a nasty noun sitting dangerously close to a hot adjective or a sizzling verb can taste like five-alarm chili in your mouth." (You can't make this stuff up.)

The most advanced of Keesling's steps is to practice what she calls sexual "bad libs," which the reader can use as a script with her partner in bed. Some examples from the book:

1. Your (noun) makes me so (adj.).
2. Stick your (adj.) (noun) in my (adj.) (noun)!
3. I need to feel your (adj.) (adj.) (noun) inside my (adj.) (adj.) (noun).
4. (Verb) me like a (adj.) (adj.) animal!

As gut-wrenchingly awkward as this advice is, it's still better than that given by 1995's *Mars and Venus in the Bedroom*. This self-help gem comes from John Gray, the same guy who wrote 1993's best-selling *Men Are from*

Mars, Women Are from Venus. Gray's theory about why heterosexual couples aren't having good sex is because men and women are hardwired to have such different desires and communication styles that they might as well be from different planets. Every piece of his advice stems from the notion that women don't let men have sex with them enough and that men don't provide enough emotional support to women for them to want to have sex. "Just as a woman needs love to open up to sex, a man needs sex to open up to love," he writes, offering tips for how to negotiate this conflict, including that couples add "quickies" (aka brief sexual encounters where the woman doesn't cum) to their sexual routines so that a man's needs can be met without a woman having to put in too much effort.

The problems with Gray's advice are innumerable, but the first is that men and women are, in point of fact, *not* from two different planets. The reason why his heterosexual female readers are not enjoying their sex lives and are buying these books in the first place is not because they are from Venus, some distant celestial body where people are inherently unable to desire sex or orgasm. It is because on planet Earth, where we all live, there are social inequities that cause a power imbalance in the bedroom (or living room, back of the minivan, wherever), which makes it difficult and sometimes impossible for women to see themselves as a protagonist in sexual scenarios and have a vocabulary to express that.

While one can argue that giving women advice on

how to better enjoy sex is a feminist move, where Keesling's and Gray's tips fail is that they encourage women to accommodate to the heteronormative narrative of men's taste and behavior, instead of attempting to help them restabilize this underlying sexual power imbalance. They do not give women a vocabulary of "dirty talk" of their own. As one paper on men's and women's sex talk from 1994 put it, "The domination of male culture over female, through such things as media representations of heterosexual relations . . . ensures that women see themselves to some extent through men's eyes. Women have no discourses with which to speak about female sexuality and female desire."

This 1994 paper was written by a trio of psychologists named June Crawford, Susan Kippax, and Catherine Waldby (henceforth CKW). They conducted a study about the differences between how men and women talk about their sexual encounters and what these disparate speech styles say about Western sexual culture at large. For the study, CKW collected and analyzed nineteen separate all-female and all-male group discussions of sex experiences from their past. Many of the conversations included stories of awkward dates and first-time fondling, but some of the most interesting data came from men and women recounting very similar interactions with wildly different takeaways.

In one of the discussions CKW analyzed, a man named Ian recalls a story from his teenage years when he and two friends picked up a group of girls at the

cyclops, panty puppet, bald-headed bastard

beach. Ian describes having wanted to pair off with a girl who ended up going with one of his friends. To his disappointment, Ian was instead "left with this fat thing" (another girl) while his buddies "wandered away."

Another discussion CKW collected was a separate but very similar story from a woman (let's call her Amy) about a time she and her friends, age sixteen, were hit on at the beach. One of Amy's friends, Helen, could tell the guy she ended up with didn't like her: "Ken was told that he could go with Helen . . . he didn't seem too pleased about it," Amy recalls. "Helen felt very embarrassed, she didn't know what to do . . . she didn't say much—the others told Ken that Helen liked him but that only seemed to make things worse . . . Helen felt that Ken believed that he had been allocated a totally unattractive social misfit."

Beyond the similarity of the two circumstances (the beach, the pickup), what these stories share is that the woman in question has no voice; her feelings are conveyed to the man by other people, if at all. Meanwhile, the man is expected to take the active role. He's expected to be the initiator, the expert, and the girl is expected to go along with whatever he decides to do. In the latter story, both Amy and Helen wonder about Ken's feelings, but never once in Ian's account does he mention how the girl might have felt. Her humanity is so irrelevant, in fact, that he refers to her as a "thing."

And yet, even though the women in these stories (Helen, Amy, and likely the unnamed girl from Ian's story) feel as though they understand the guys' points of view, they do not attempt to share that out loud. They don't say, "Hey! I can tell you're not into me, and— good news—I'm not into you either, so how about we just don't put ourselves through this, okay?" Instead, they follow the (unfortunate) unspoken rules of these sorts of interactions, which say the woman must "accept her status as object." Her fate is determined by what the guy chooses to do. And according to our cultural standards of heterosexual masculinity and male sex drive, he is expected to want the sex and to pursue it, whether either of them actually wants it or not.

The narratives of male and female desire that most of us grow up with say that it isn't possible for a woman to want sex without also wanting some sort of commitment. That's relevant because as CKW point out, it could be part of the reason why in casual sex scenarios, a dude so often fails to connect with what the woman wants. With her humanity. Sometimes he does, but that's the exception. "Men seem to feel an obligation for commitment if they relate to their female partner as a person," CKW determine. "She may be content with a one-night stand, but would prefer it to be with someone to whom she can relate person-to-person as well as body-to-body." (Which seems fairly reasonable to me? Again, is this why lesbian sex is better?) Yet, it appears that on the whole, men often relate to women person-to-person only within ongoing relationships, not casual sex. Whether it be because the culture has taught him that all women are stage-four

cyclops, panty puppet, bald-headed bastard

clingers or that his orgasm is the only real goal, a dude in a hookup scenario might unconsciously feel he must treat the woman like an object, or else he'll trap himself into a serious dating situation instead of simply, I don't know, becoming better at sex.

CKW conclude their study with this vision for the future:

> A discourse of sex as pleasure, separating pleasure from procreation, and acknowledging women as active desiring and sexually assertive subjects, not necessarily centered around the erect penis, will challenge and confront estab-lished power structures. What is needed is a new mythology, one which speaks about mutual exploration, communication, discovery, and pleasuring one another, where penetration is not an end unto itself, but one of the many possi-bilities for erotic enjoyment.

A big part of that new mythology is surely a reimag-ined lexicon of sex (a *sexicon*!) that allows people who aren't cisgender dudes to talk about their bodies and de-sires from their own perspectives. In some communities, that lexicon is already being invented, and it starts where this chapter started: with what we call our genitalia.

Lal Zimman has devoted a great deal of research to observing how self-identifying your own junk on your terms can be sexually empowering. His work has focused specifically on transgender communities, who take the challenge of genitalia renaming one step further by calling into question what we consider male and female bodies in the first place. To a trans person (one who hasn't had gender confirmation surgery*), a doctor or dictionary might classify their bodies one way; but when you consider what we learned back in chapter 2 about the cultural baggage we bring when interpreting a person's body, the logic behind that black-and-white classification starts to unravel.

If someone identifies as a woman even though they were assigned male at birth, can't they call their junk a *pussy* if they want to, even if a physician might call it a *penis*? Can't they use the language that feels most comfortable and affirming to describe their own bodies?

As Zimman's research has revealed, they can, and they do. He has carefully studied trans folks' genital naming practices by looking at them in their most explicit, unfiltered state: on the internet—specifically in chat rooms, forums, and Craigslist hookup ads. In practice, trans people often use genital terminology that breaks the link that usually exists between gender and genitalia. If you look at dictionary definitions, they'll typically list a description of a body part's function and make a connection to the gender it "goes with" (e.g.,

cyclops, panty puppet, bald-headed bastard

* Formerly known as "sex reassignment surgery."

"The part of the genital canal in the female"). What trans people often do, however, is select only one of those semantic elements when talking about their own bodies.

The folks Zimman studied sometimes used both normatively male and normatively female terminology, depending on the context—and that included more technical terms, like *vagina* and *clitoris*, as well as vernacular terms like *dick* and *pussy*. "When they use traditionally female terminology, they're referring to the structure," Zimman explains, referencing these quotes from trans guys: "I'm not the only one who's filled with hatred over his vagina, am I?"; "I feel utter revulsion toward my vagina"; and "I hate the idea of vaginal/anal penetration, and I tried to explain that I'm not a virgin and that I've just never had vagina sex before 'cause I'm just not comfortable with that."

What's more common is for people to follow the opposite pattern and use slangy male terminology to refer to body parts that would normatively be seen as female, and same for slangy female terminology to talk about normatively male parts. In the first season of the Amazon TV series *I Love Dick*, a female character named Toby performs oral sex on an androgynous character named Devon, who has what a doctor would probably call a vagina; but as Toby is doing her thing down there, she refers to Devon's junk as a *cock*. Trans YouTuber Alex Bertie does something similar, referring to what's between his legs as a *dick*, even though he hasn't had any surgery.

Using slang to self-identify their own genitalia is a go-to move for trans folks. "A lot of trans people now see a male body as a body belonging to anyone who identifies as a man," says Zimman. And vice versa for a female body. In some cases, they might even hybridize words to create brand-new ones—*boycunt*, *manpussy*, and *dicklit* are a few Zimman has come across. Using these words is an act of "reclaiming the body parts themselves," Zimman says. "It's part of a general reframing of these body parts that are so often a source of discomfort, of dysphoria, of rejection—it's reframing them as something that is erotic and . . . that doesn't necessarily have to involve erasing the differences that exist in trans bodies."

What we stand to learn here is that evidently, if one decides they don't feel like *vagina*, *box*, *snatch*, *boning*, or *screwing* most accurately or comfortably describe their bodies or sex, they can chuck our current sexicon out the window. They can come up with their own entirely new words. In 2015, I asked a bunch of my cisgender women friends if they could rename their equipment anything they wanted to, what would it be? Their responses ranged from silly to saucy, including terms like *galaxy*, *pooka*, *freya*, *V*, *vashina*, and *peach*. The delightfully comprehensive phrase *vaginal-cliteral-vulval complex* (or VCVC) is another women-invented term I've heard to describe said genitalia.

wordslut

I also did a little research online to find out what trans and queer communities call their bodies when they want something gender neutral that's a little more fun than *genitalia*. Thanks to Tumblr, I discovered *stuff, junk, bits, down there, front hole, funparts, venis,* and *click*.

I don't expect the complete dissolution of the words *vagina* or *penis* or their problematic slang alternatives. But I'm into the idea of inviting women and gender-queer folks to describe sex and their bodies however they like, regardless of what medical professionals, movies, or porn tell them to say. We could start by using our words of choice just with sexual partners, then move on to using them with our friends in the real world, then bring them to the internet, and eventually, who knows? Maybe, little by little, the intention behind them will sink into the cultural consciousness, until one day, calling a vagina a *VCVC* and sex *sheathing* will be just as common as saying *snatch* and *screwing*. Maybe the idea of naming your own body on your terms will catch on. And maybe when that happens, a rebalancing of the sexual power scales will finally follow.

There are a lot of maybes and who knows in that sentiment. As always, predictions when it comes to the relationship between language and social change are notoriously hard to make. Still, it is part of a researcher's job to make hypotheses. So, to come full circle, I asked the trusted experts I spoke to for this book to give their brutally honest insight about the future of the English language, not only with regard to sex, but to everything: insults, gender and sexuality labels, grammar, catcalling, cursing. Deborah Cameron, Lal Zimman, and a few others have some pretty mind-blowing ideas.

so ... in one thousand years, will women rule the english language?

ENGLISH DICTIONARY

In 1987 a duo of kooky hardcore feminists named Mary Daly and Jane Caputi published a book called *Websters' First New Intergalactic Wickedary of the English Language*. This radical, lady-powered new dictionary was aimed at transforming English, or what they labeled "patriarchal speech," into a language for and about women.

Daly and Caputi were the kinds of die-hard second-wave feminists who genuinely believed that women were the intellectually and morally superior gender and that a world helmed by them should be our realistic goal. (They were the kinds of feminists that many political right-wingers think are the *only* kind.)

Daly and Caputi's iconoclastic *Wickedary* redefined and tweaked old English words, and introduced new ones, to create a wacky, witchy new language that ostensibly reflected the world as women saw it. Here are a few notable entries:

DICK-TIONARY: Any patriarchal dictionary; a derivative, tamed and muted lexicon compiled by dicks.

HAG: A Witch, Fury, Harpy who haunts the Hedges/ Boundaries of patriarchy, frightening fools and summoning Weird Wandering Women to the Wild.

CRONE-OLOGY: Radical Feminist chronology.

GYN/ECOLOGY: Knowledge enabling Crones to expose connections among institutions, ideologies, and atrocities.

Lots of new feminist dictionaries, or "dyketionaries" as they were often called, began popping up around this time in the 1970s and '80s, though the *Wickedary* was surely the most famous. The authors' idea was that if we could redefine the English language to reflect how women see the world, we could redefine the world itself too. That's not really how language works, but Daly and Caputi weren't the only feminists who thought English as we know it was fundamentally failing women. In 1980 feminist scholar Dale Spender published a book called *Man Made Language*, and in it she made the argument that since the English language was created by men, it expresses an exclusively male point of view, which through osmosis brainwashes women into thinking men's perspectives are the only ones that matter or even exist. Thus, we need a reimagined, woman-made version of English to reverse this way of thinking.

Logic like Spender's was what many second-wave activists anticipated would guide the English language forward, helping progress toward gender equality in general along its way. Spender's book reflects one interpretation of a principle known as the Sapir-Whorf hypothesis, which was proposed in the early twentieth century to explain the effects that a language has on its speakers' worldview. There are two versions of this principle: the lighter (more widely accepted) one says that language merely *influences* thought, while the strong one (with which Spender's theory aligns) says that language *determines* thought. By Spender's account, the grammar and vocabulary of your native tongue inherently shape your perception of reality—if there isn't a word to describe a certain concept in your language, then you can't conceive of that thing at all. And since English dictionaries and grammar were made up by men, women need to invent a whole new language that puts their view of the world at the center.

Perhaps the most admirable attempt (and biggest failure) at feminist language reform came a few years after Spender's book, when linguist Suzette Haden Elgin tried to invent a whole new "women's language" to replace English. In 1984 Elgin published a sci-fi dystopian novel called *Native Tongue*, which, much like Margaret Atwood's *The Handmaid's Tale*, is set in a postapocalyptic future where American women have no rights, only serve one societal purpose (to bear and rear children), and are completely at the mercy of their husbands and fathers. There is one exception in the *Native Tongue* universe: a special group of female linguists, who get to work outside the home as interpreters and facilitate communication with the aliens that have now made contact with Earth (not dissimilar from the 2016 Amy Adams movie *Arrival*). In their free time, these female linguists collaborate in secret to create a brand-new language called Láadan, which expresses the worldview of women only. Using this novel communication system, they plan to dethrone the patriarchy and free themselves from enslavement once and for all.

With Láadan, Suzette Haden Elgin went way further than Daly and Caputi's *Wickedary*; she made up a fully functioning language, like Klingon from *Star Trek*, but even more intense. Láadan was complete with a fleshed-out grammatical structure (among its features were certain modifiers that allowed speakers to clearly state their

emotional intentions, which Elgin thought seemed inherently female), a sound system (including tones, like
in Mandarin Chinese—Deborah Cameron thinks Elgin
did this not for feminist reasons but instead because she
simply "thought they were neat"), and a small core vocabulary. Elgin wanted the Láadan lexicon to include words
that efficiently summed up what she thought to be common physical, social, and emotional experiences shared
by women, which were otherwise unspoken or would
take multiple convoluted sentences in English to describe. For example, in Láadan, there are distinct words
meaning "to menstruate early," "to menstruate painfully,"
and "to menstruate joyfully." There are words differenti-
ating the nuances between frustration and anger both
with reason and without reason, both with someone to
blame and without someone to blame. There is a verb
doroledim, describing the act of a woman overeating to
cope with a lack of ability to care for herself properly
while at the same time feeling extreme guilt about over-
indulging in something as gluttonous as food. There is a
noun *radiidin*, which translates to "a non-holiday," or an
occasion generally thought to be a holiday but is actually
a burden due to women having to cook, decorate, and
prepare for so many guests single-handedly. These are
just a few words from the over 1,800-entry vocabulary that
describe what Elgin conceived to be distinctly women-
known phenomena.

Elgin didn't create Láadan for sheer entertainment;
she sincerely hoped, and speculated, that it would have

real-world political consequences. "My hypothesis," she told an interviewer in 2007, "was that if I constructed a language designed specifically to provide a more adequate mechanism for expressing women's perceptions, women would (a) embrace it and begin using it, or (b) embrace the idea but not the language . . . and construct some other 'women's language' to replace it."

Obviously, neither of those things happened in the years after *Native Tongue*. Láadan and its nifty tones and quirky vocabulary did not replace or even make an impression on English speakers. Neither did any of the dyketionaries that were written during that time. There are inherent problems with the idea of a singular "women's language." As Deborah Cameron comments, "I was always skeptical about the idea of a language 'expressing women's perceptions.' Which perceptions would those be, and which women would they belong to? There is no set of perceptions which all women share." As nice as it is to believe in a collective sisterhood, women's experiences make up a complex spectrum, and "sisterhood" doesn't mean just one thing.

These failed attempts at replacing dicktionaries with dyketionaries serve as evidence that the English language is, in fact, *not* inherently patriarchal. Pragmatically speaking, we don't actually need to altogether reinvent the English language, no matter who wrote the grammar guides. As we've discovered, women are unbelievably innovative linguistically—from their slang to their word pronunciation—and can wield their existing

English to express themselves just fine. Not to mention, making a language feminist does not start with making the vowels, consonants, or even vocabulary feminist. It starts with transforming the ideologies of its speakers.

Daly, Caputi, Elgin, and Spender's vision for the English language assumed that changing how one speaks would change their politics. It was an optimistic theory. But Lal Zimman reminds us that isn't the order in which things occur. "Anytime language reform happens, it has to happen in the context of cultural change," he says. "You can't have just the linguistic change first and then expect people to get on board with the cultural stuff."

Those women did get a few important things right, however. For one, they managed to successfully highlight a general androcentrism that continues to exist in the making of formal language guides, due to the simple fact that jobs in lexicography, grammar, and the like were historically only available to men. (For example, did you know the word *lesbian* was not added to the *Oxford English Dictionary* until 1976? Incredibly, when it finally did get an entry, the following treasure from writer Cecil Day-Lewis was included as the example sentence: "I shall never write real poetry. Women never do, unless they're invalids, or Lesbians, or something.")

Women like Elgin and Spender also accurately deduced that language is an enormous part of social reform. It's no coincidence that *Native Tongue*, the *Wickedary*, and Robin Lakoff's *Language and Woman's Place* were published during the second-wave feminist movement. During that highly political era, social empowerment inspired linguistic empowerment.

But interest in gender and language reform ebbs and flows. Zimman says that in the early 2000s, when he was applying to grad school and wanted to talk about transgender identity and linguistics, nobody cared. By then, people had decided the topic was too niche, not applicable. But ten or fifteen years later, issues of gender and sexual equality began rising to the cultural front lines again, and so did the language we use to talk about them.

However, as feminist voices become louder, indicating that a social and linguistic revolution is coming, the voices of their opposers crescendo too. "We're really seeing that this new progress narrative of marching toward a better world for all oppressed people is not going to work out as simply as people thought," Zimman told me one foggy day in Santa Barbara. "With these social changes comes pushback."

This conversation with Zimman was my last interview for this book—it happened at the end of December 2017 as the Thomas Fire, one of the largest wildfires in modern California history, blazed through the hills behind us, burning thousands of acres to the ground and filling the air with ash. "The more we move in a direction of respecting nonnormative identities and a language that goes along with that, the more dramatic the pushback is going to be," Zimman said.

My last question for Zimman, one that I posed to

Deborah Cameron as well, was about what we can realistically expect for the future of English. How long will it take for gender-neutral pronouns to become a natural part of everyday speech? Can we really invent a new vocabulary of feminist curse words? Will we ever stop hating on how young women and gay men talk? Will catcalling and slut-shaming ever disappear?

Cameron predicts it's going to be a bumpy road. "I think gender-neutral pronouns—or at least, one of them, *they*—will spread. It's already in the system. But I don't think misogynistic language will become any less common," she wrote to me from Oxford. "This is a time when unfortunately misogyny is on the rise, and in this area, usage typically reflects the overall cultural mood. Misogyny won't go unopposed but will continue."

Even Adam Szetela, a feminist scholar at Boston's Berklee College of Music (an idyllic liberal enclave chock-a-block with eighteen-year-old acoustic guitar prodigies), thinks we're in for a rough ride. "With regard to feminist language change, I think there will be—as there already is—a backlash to this progress," he told me, reasoning that the conservative right and its "far-right stepbrother" will remain steadfast in their fight to prevent the mainstreaming of feminist values in the English language. Szetela thinks Donald Trump's presidency in particular has had a regressive effect that will take some years to reverse. "While in certain spheres, language that was once okay is being ousted as problematic, the most powerful person in the world is modeling sexism on a routine basis . . . [with] no consequences," he wrote to me in December 2017. "Thus, the message to young men coming of age in the era of Trump is that this is a socially acceptable way of relating to, interacting with, and speaking about women."

I've seen both sides of this trend—the positive language reform and the ensuing counterblast—show up in places as innocuous as UrbanDictionary.com, the popular online slang inventory. The specific entry that comes to mind is for the word *mansplain*. This popular slang term was first invented thanks to a 2008 essay by prolific author Rebecca Solnit. The essay told of a time when Solnit was forced to endure a strange man at a party patronizingly explaining the content of a history book to her, failing to let her get a word in edgewise to let him know that she, in fact, had written it. Solnit didn't coin *mansplain* personally; the word first appeared in a comment on LiveJournal a month after her essay was published, and it subsequently exploded in use, first among bloggers, then the mainstream media, then everyday conversation. *Mansplain* was a beautiful portmanteau that filled a gap in the English language, describing a concept that so many women are familiar with but for which a word had not previously existed. It became such a sensation that in 2010, the *New York Times* named it one of their words of the year. Naturally, it was soon entered onto UrbanDictionary.com.

And yet, if you were to look up Urban Dictionary's top entries for *mansplain* (at least at the time I'm writing this), they do not reflect the original. Anyone can enter a word onto Urban Dictionary; its contents are 100 percent crowdsourced, and the top definitions are voted on by its users. Theoretically, this has democratized how we document and define words. But sometimes, things go awry. The top three most upvoted definitions for *mansplain* read as follows:

1. **Basically when a man explains something to a woman and gets chastised for it. Seriously, you can't make this shit up if you tried.**
2. **When women explain things to men in a condescending attitude.**
3. **Feminist [sic] talking down to men just because they are men.**

If I had to wager a guess, I'd predict these definitions were written by men who felt strongly and instantly attacked by women's newfound ability to express what it felt like to be mansplained to, and who preferred to villainize women over listening to them. To me, their entries are proof that women (or any oppressed group) can come up with new words to express what were once unnamed experiences, but sometimes the backlash is louder than the progress.

That might all sound depressing, but linguists are still optimistic that positive shifts forward are imminent. After all, even if Urban Dictionary's definition of *mansplain* is a step in the wrong direction, I found the word a few months later on Merriam-Webster.com and its entry reassuringly read: "to explain something to a woman in a condescending way that assumes she has no knowledge about the topic" (which much more accurately reflects the original meaning).

Historically, the English language has also seen progressive movements on a larger scale—an encouraging sign for the future. "Languages go in a more feminist direction when there's widespread support for feminism (as in the 1970s, say)," Cameron told me, "so what we can do is keep on fighting for feminism in general, and refuse to be silenced."

A big part of that refusal, according to Zimman, means understanding the inherent politics reflected in our language use and in the linguistic studies currently being conducted. "We can't just pretend to be doing dispassionate linguistics and not recognize that these things are already extremely political and that we may even have a responsibility to those politics," Zimman says. "I think there's an overall move . . . to taking responsibility for the implications of what we're doing." In other words, like in the 1970s, academia and activism are merging, and this can be really powerful.

But we're not all academics. In my personal opinion, one of the most meaningful things the rest of us everyday folks can do amid so much political pushback is to move through life with the confident knowledge that every persecuted element of our speech—the hedges, the upspeak, the lisps, the vocal fry—is there for a logical, powerful, and provable reason. When someone tries to question your voice or use sexist words against you, knowing exactly what is motivating them to do so and why it's misinformed could help you open up a dialogue with them, which in my experience is an amazing icebreaker even if you otherwise have very little in common. Everybody inherently wants to know why people talk the way they do, and if you have some information about that, they're likely to listen.

I was once at a friend's backyard barbecue where this one guest, a guy in his early thirties wearing a gray suit and a nice watch, began telling the group about a woman on a news show he was watching earlier that day. He said she was messing up her side of the debate because she kept saying "you know, you know, you know" over and over, and it sounded like she didn't know what she was talking about. "I would have listened to her if she'd have just quit it with that," he said. And when he did, it reminded me of the Upper East Side mom who chastised me for saying "y'all" back in college.

"I actually know a little something about the phrase *you know*," I interjected. I then proceeded to tell this guy how *you know* is not just a mindless filler, but rather a discourse marker with a purpose. I told him about how women actually use it to display confidence a lot of time, and how hedges generally work as essential tools for creating trust and empathy in controversial conversations but are often misinterpreted because of cultural myths about women, self-assuredness, and authority.

"To tell the truth, I've heard you use *you know* maybe a dozen times tonight," I told the guy with a smile. "It's not a bad thing."

After I finished my little spiel about *you know*, this guy looked at me with these sort of big, surprised eyes and said, completely genuinely, might I add, "Wow, it's cool you know so much about how people talk. You must be the most interesting person in every room."

I am certainly *not* the most interesting person in any room (and thank goodness for that). But my point in telling this story is that language can be a really useful entry point—a horizontally oriented topic, if you will—to talk about larger ideas of gender equality, especially if you're armed with cool, nerdy facts like the usage patterns and social utility of *you know*.

The ultimate goal is to avoid at all costs the dystopian patriarchal future depicted in *Native Tongue*—to move our culture little by little in the opposite direction. "Overall, I'm optimistic," Lal Zimman tells me over the phone with a wistful cheer. "I think the culture is changing in a way that will result in more good things for people who need good things."

I can tell Zimman and I are cut from the same cloth in this way—just a couple of wide-eyed language geeks who believe with our whole hearts (and brains) that change is just around the corner. "I *have* to be optimistic, to make it through," he says with a laugh. "You have to believe that it's possible."

acknowledgments

Sometimes I get so giddy that a whole slew of smart, accomplished people agreed to let me write this book that it makes me feel like my internal organs might implode. First, I need to thank my sensational superhero agent, Rachel Vogel at Dunow, Carlson, and Lerner, for taking a chance on me, guiding me, talking me up when I was too far down, down when I was too far up, and straight-up changing my life forever. Next, my editors at Harper Wave: the masterful Karen Rinaldi and astute Rebecca Raskin, who whipped me into shape and pushed me to turn a jumble of half thoughts and internet-y jokes into a real book, teaching me skills I'll carry with me forever. My gratitude overflows.

To my parents, world-class scientists Craig and Denise Montell, for always believing hardcore in their wild card of a daughter and letting me follow my wacky dreams.

Thank you for the genetic gift of tenacity, for setting an example for how to work hard (and play harder), and for always making me feel like you're proud of me. It's mutual, I promise.

To my little (but tall) brother, the scarily intelligent Google software engineer Brandon Montell, for making me feel so sibling-rivalrous that I had to write a book just to feel like I had a shot in hell of competing with your mind and achievements.

To my smart, luminous, encouraging friends, especially Rachel Wiegand (thanks for reading early drafts of this thing, dude). This might be cringey, but I also want to shout out the Instagram followers who messaged me and cheered me on as I posted throughout my writing process—those DMs seriously meant the world.

To my many creative mentors and spirit guides, including Kerri Kolen (whom I think of as this book's "birth mom"), Sarah Murphy, Saïd Sayrafiezadeh, Brett Paesel, Rebecca Odes, and Jill Soloway, who when I was twenty-two years old believed I had something to say to the world with basically no evidence that that was true and gave me a space to do it. I am in awe and so, so thankful.

To my supportive bosses at Clique, who let me take six months off my job to write this thing and welcomed me back with open arms.

To my gifted photographer pal Katie Neuhof for taking my author photo and to L.A. designer Anine Bing for dressing me in those nifty threads for it.

To my talented illustrator, Rose Wong, for making these chapters look so sparkly and special.

And finally, to the mind-bendingly brilliant linguists who talked to me for this book, especially Lal Zimman, Deborah Cameron, Sonja Lanehart, and my former NYU professor Louise O. Vasvári, who introduced me to the topic of language and gender in the first place. My linguistics degree was supposed to be impractical, but damn, it worked out. I am so grateful it hurts. Thank you, thank you, thank you.

acknowledgments

about the author

AMANDA MONTELL is a writer and reporter from Baltimore with a BA in linguistics from New York University. Her favorite English word is *nook* and her favorite foreign word is *tartle*, the Scottish term for the moment you go to introduce someone but realize you have forgotten their name. Amanda lives in Los Angeles. This is her first book.